AUTHOR YOUR LIFE

How One Writer Changed Her Life Through the Power of
Storytelling and How You Can, Too

LARA ZIELIN

Sparklepen Industries

Contents

Also by Lara Zielin

Young Adult Fiction

Donut Days

The Implosion of Aggie Winchester

The Waiting Sky

Young Adult Nonfiction

Make Things Happen: The Key to Networking for Teens

Romance (written as Kim Amos)

A Kiss to Build a Dream On

And Then He Kissed Me

Every Little Kiss

One More Kiss

AUTHOR YOUR LIFE

Copyright 2019 by Lara Zielin

Sparklepen Industries

To all of you out there daring to believe
a better story is possible,
I got you.

Let's do this.

Introduction

This story begins where all good stories begin—in Wisconsin. This beginning is also a ghost story, so this book is pretty much batting a thousand right now.

What happened was this: Two kids were driving west on Wisconsin back roads in the pitch-black dead of night. Think two a.m. Starless. Spooky. And they were the only car for miles.

This was, of course, when the passenger (let's call her Jane) told the driver (let's call him Ted) that she had to pee. *Pick your spot*, Ted said, motioning with his hand to the inky black woods all around them, *the world is your toilet*. To be fair, Ted didn't say this. My father-in-law says *the world is your toilet* when he's in the woods. It's a phrase I sometimes can't get out of my head.

Anyway.

Jane would have loved for Ted to just pull alongside the deserted road so she could pee in the woods, except she couldn't because she used a cane. And the way her body and her plumbing worked, squatting in the woods just wasn't an option. Our girl needed a proper toilet. So Ted put the pedal to the metal and kept hoping they'd come upon something—anything—that was open. And lo, they did.

The Roadhouse Bar in Hawthorne, Wisconsin, blazed bright in the night. Lights on. Music playing. Ted and Jane were overjoyed. They had heard locals talking about the bar because an artist, rumored to be from Disney, had just painted an enormous mural on the walls of the place.

They went in. Jane did her business. Ted bought them beers. And that's when they noticed things seemed a little…off.

The jukebox kept playing the same song, "Let's Twist Again" by Chubby Checker, over and over. People wouldn't stop *staring* at them.

Jane told Ted she was unnerved. Ted told her everything was cool, and that they should take a closer look at this neato new mural. It was a saloon scene with gunfighters and poker players, with painted ladies on stage and a sheriff about to draw his weapon. There was a shootout in the dusty streets, and a bartender serving people amid the chaos.

That's when Ted and Jane noticed that everyone in the bar looked like someone in the mural. The men playing pool in the bar looked like the men at the gambling table in the mural; the guy next to the jukebox in the bar looked like the guy next to the player piano; the women sipping drinks at the bar looked like the corseted ladies on stage…on and on.

Of course, it was easy to explain. The local artist

who'd painted the scenes had surely drawn from real life and used local folks as character inspiration. Ted figured he'd ask about it, so as he bought two more beers, he inquired with the bartender: "Did the artist who painted that mural use you guys here as inspiration?"

The bartender, a younger man, didn't reply. He just smiled and sort of nodded vaguely. Like he couldn't quite understand what Ted was saying. This was about the time "Let's Twist Again" was on its umpteenth repeat, and Jane was starting to get wigged the eff out. Both she and Ted suddenly realized that the people at the bar had drinks, but didn't seem to be actually drinking them. Men stood by the pool table, but didn't actually play.

Jane wanted to go, but Ted insisted they finish their beers. So they studied the mural a little more, and that's when they saw it. Something that hadn't been there before. Behind the saloon doors in the corner of a gun-slinging scene were two pairs of legs. And next to one of them was a cane.

Jane's hair stood up on the back of her neck. Those were her legs, and that was *her cane*. She realized she and Ted were being drawn into the mural. *In real time*.

Naturally, they freaked out and ran from the place as fast as they could. The minute they exited the Road-house, all the lights went off. Everything went silent. They sped away, not saying anything. Figuring that maybe they imagined the whole thing.

Eventually, when they calmed down a few days later, curiosity overtook them. What had happened that night? It was surely explainable. So they went back to figure out what went down.

When they returned, it was a busy night, packed with folks and music—though thankfully not "Let's Twist Again." Jane and Ted sidled up to the bar and asked who was working the other night around two a.m. They described the young bartender who had served them, to which the *current* bartender said, "No one like that works here."

Naw, naw, naw, Jane and Ted insisted. *That was our boy. We saw him.*

To which the current bartender said, "My dad and I own this place. We are the only people who bartend. And that night? We locked up at midnight."

I heard this story on season one of the *Spooked* podcast, hosted by Glynn Washington, and I recommend that you go listen to it because the narrator does a much better job of actually, you know, *telling the story* than I do of recreating it here.

So why bother sharing the story at all?

The short answer is, when I heard this episode of *Spooked*, I was changed. (The long answer is this entire book, so there's that.) I was like Saul on the Road to Damascus *altered*.

What I realized was that something about the mural had impacted reality for Jane and Ted. The artist's creation of the saloon scene had, in some way, brought forth that art into actual real life. The fabric of time and space had been altered that night...because of a painting.

Art is powerful. It changes hearts and minds all the time. I get that. But this was the first time I had considered whether art could literally change the course of things—if it was powerful enough to create an entirely new reality that we humans could actually experience.

And while I'm not an artist like that Disney guy, I am a writer. My art is books. So I was like, *listen*, if a Disney guy can open up a damn time warp with a weird saloon mural, maybe I can impact my life by writing a book about how I *want* the story of my life to turn out and then see if it will actually *turn out that way*.

As a writer, I'm always considering what my characters want. I'm always asking what their motivations are. What will make them happy? What is a satisfying story for them? But I had never really considered the story of my own life. What was *my* motivation? What would make *me* happy?

Elizabeth Gilbert, the best-selling author of the books *Big Magic* and *Eat, Pray, Love*, posits that our creative muses whisper to us all the time to give us ideas and energy to cheerlead our work bringing forth the art that's inside of us.

My hypothesis, and the foundation for this book, is essentially to ask: What if our muses—or, say, God or the Universe or divine energy or whatever you want to call it—speak to us not just about art, but about our lives? Like, what if we have our own story, our own real-life *life*, that is ready to break through, to be created, and we just have to access it and write it into reality?

What if we stopped asking what our characters want, and started asking, "What do I want?" And then what if we wrote that down into a bomb-ass story that we told about ourselves?

So that's what I did.

Starting January 1, 2018, I decided to give myself a year of writing a book I very unimaginatively titled *Lara's Life*. Every day I wrote pages about what happened in *Lara's life*. Every day I sat down and imagined what would make Lara happy and fulfilled.

Writing her like a character, I put her in situations that were amazing and awesome. I fixed her heart, which was getting more than a little brittle and hard. I gave her more compassion for people. I gave her abundance—of time, of money, of love. I gave her a great sex life and a healthier weight. And I gave her joy. Tons of joy. Truck-fulls of joy. Which is something real-life Lara (that's me!) had let dribble out of her, kind of like a slow leak over time that you don't realize is happening, until one day you wake up and you can almost see a gray film on your life that colors everything sad.

I hand-wrote *Lara's Life* old school, in notebooks I filled up, page after page, pouring out my soul. Imagining what life could be like for this "character."

Now, almost a year later, I'm on the other side of that process.

And holy shit, you guys. IT HAS TOTALLY WORKED. This is real AF.

The changes started almost right away, though I'm not going to lie and tell you this is a quick fix or something because the big stuff—the really important stuff—

took time. But any good book takes time. You don't just sit down and finish a book in two weeks. Well, I guess you could, but it's probably not going to be any good if you do.

Author Your Life is what happened when I wrote the story of how I wanted my existence to be. When I dared to create a world for myself, the same way I would spend time and energy creating a world for my characters. It's what I learned, it's what I experienced, it's where I was broken and healed, cracked open and then filled up again.

Author Your Life is how this whole thing went down for me. And now *Author Your Life* is also how you can do this same thing for yourself and write the story of your existence the way you want it to happen, and then *watch it happen*.

So hold on to your butts. And get out your pens.

It's time to write your story.

AWARENESS

ONE

You Can Write a Better Story for Yourself

What if I could tell you what was going to happen to you?

Better yet, what if *you* knew what was going to happen to you, and you even directed the outcome?

I'm not a psychic and I can't read the stars, but I do know one thing: How stories work. And all of us here on planet Earth are living, walking, breathing stories.

The stories that we love and tell over and over all have a beginning, a middle, and an end, and roughly same thing happens to the protagonist each time in the big scheme of things—from Luke Skywalker in *Star Wars* to Beca in *Pitch Perfect*. That might sound a little bananas since one of them flies a space ship and fights the Dark Side, while another joins an *a capella* group. But the stages of their transformation? Totally the same.

This blueprint for storytelling is called the Hero's Journey, and it was popularized by a mythologist named Joseph Campbell in the 1970s. He researched the crap out of stories across time and cultures and, turns out, they're all made out of pretty much the same scaffolding. From the stories carved into the side of a cave to the singing and dancing in *Hamilton*—they are all using the Hero's Journey.

At the start of 2018, when I wanted to change my life, I decided to do it through the power of storytelling. At the time, I knew I was unhappy, though I'm not sure I really grasped the full extent of it. Here's what I can say about January 1, 2018, when I started my own Hero's Journey:

First, I woke up the heaviest weight I'd been in years. Actually, probably the heaviest I'd ever been. I can't tell you what I ate that day, but I can definitely tell you I drank. Because drinking was something I found myself doing more and more.

I'm not sure what my husband Rob and I did that day, but I can tell you what we *didn't* do—we didn't have sex. We were close but hadn't been intimate in a long while. My work writing novels, which had once been thriving, had also dried up, leaving me questioning who in the world I was since I'd only wanted to be a novelist. Ever. It felt inextricably linked to my identity, and I was shuffling around, lost, without it.

And while I had a well-paying part-time job that kept a regular paycheck coming in and ensured we had things like health insurance, the gigs Rob and I had started on the side—me a writing business and Rob an ice cream store—were often struggling. We were getting by, but barely.

We were living paycheck to paycheck. We were both heavy. And while we liked each other a lot, our relationship wasn't exactly thriving. I was drinking to numb all kinds of pain, though I probably couldn't have said exactly where I was hurting at the time. It just felt like a terrible ache *all over*.

I started *Lara's Life* as an experiment, a way to test whether writing about the life I wanted could actually help it come to pass.

And right after I started, everything that I wanted to have happen came true immediately and it was super easy, THE END!

Haha, no.

What a boring story that would be if everything just fell into place and I didn't have to change at all to make my deepest desires come true. Instead, what happened was the tried and true pattern of the Hero's Journey. There were nearly predictable challenges that occurred as I worked to create a better story around my finances, my health, my relationships, and much more.

The amazing thing is that because I'd put my "life" into a story structure, I knew the challenges were coming. After all, as an author, I knew the Hero's Journey. I knew the patterns and the obstacles that would challenge the protagonist, who in this case was me.

So when I wrote about Lara having more financial abundance, I was not at all surprised when our finances shit the bed. When I wanted a better relationship with Rob, it's no surprise that we suddenly had big huge boulders in our path that we had to push out of the way.

Sounds super fun, right? Don't worry, the challenges didn't last forever, and, like any good protagonist, I learned lessons along the way. Plus, hello happy ending! I'm living, breathing proof that a willingness to go through these challenges results in the ability to come out on the other side of the experience, forever changed. And, in my case, to write this book as a result.

Think about it: In *Spider-Man: Into the Spider-Verse*, Miles Morales couldn't have taken the leap of faith to become Spider-Man if he hadn't been at his lowest point, having just lost his uncle, been kicked out of the Spider-gang, and tied to a chair. In *Pitch Perfect*, Beca couldn't have led her team to winning the *a capella* competition if she hadn't realized she'd built walls to keep people out, and then been brave enough to tear down those same walls.

But Lara, you say, Miles and Beca are fictional characters, and this is real life.

That is true! But here's the thing. The Hero's Journey is more than just the blueprint for good storytelling. Campbell himself suggested it was part of our human DNA, that there was no other way to explain its prevalence across culture and time.

I'd go a step further and posit that the Hero's Journey is a fundamental, unshakable law in the universe like gravity or the speed of light. Why? Because it's repeatable. I'd say it's even testable. When you start the Hero's Journey, the same cycle occurs. Every time.

I'd argue it's possible that humans didn't create the Hero's Journey, but that instead, humans are a *reflection* of the Hero's Journey. It's not a monomyth that formed as a result of human activity over time, and it's not something we're supposed to study for useful nuggets, simply because it IS the nugget.

This is why you won't see me referring to Jesus or Buddha or Mohammed in this book, because, like gravity, the rules of the Hero's Journey apply no matter what you believe. Instead, I use the ubiquitous term "the universe," because I treat the Hero's Journey and the truths therein as a universal law. If it helps, you can also think of this process as tapping into your human ability to recognize big, universal patterns that help you identify the things that are holding you back, and thereby to achieve your highest self.

As such, the Hero's Journey is a blueprint not just for fiction but for real-life, too. It's the roadmap for what's going to happen to you when you start creating the life that you want. It's all the cards laid out on the table, telling you step by step what to expect.

We don't inform it—it informs us. It will guide us if we let it.

And the guidance goes like this:

THE HERO'S JOURNEY

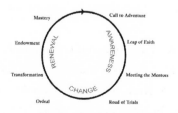

AWARENESS
  Call to Adventure
  Leap of Faith
  Meeting the Mentors
  CHANGE
  Road of Trials
  Ordeal
  RENEWAL
  Transformation
  Endowment
  Mastery

I've structured *Author Your Life* around the Hero's Journey. There are three major sections to the book—Awareness, Change, and Renewal—though, to be fair, I've spent the most time around Awareness and Change because these are the hardest parts of the journey, and the ones where we need the most help. I'm also using Awareness, Change, and Renewal in place of the more common Hero's Journey descriptors of Departure, Initiation, and Return. I read and loved the descriptions of Awareness, Change, and Renewal in a book by Will Craig called *Living the Hero's Journey: Exploring Your Role in the Action-Adventure of a Lifetime* (Live and Learn Publishing, 2017), and they are used here with permission from the author.

I've also taken the liberty to streamline our journey a bit. According to Wikipedia, there are more than 17 parts to the Hero's Journey. That's a lot of parts! My goal here isn't to dive into every single moment of the Hero's Journey in huge detail. Instead, it's to get you to recognize big, overarching patterns that can help you understand where you are in the adventure, while keeping in mind that it's a circle, and it's continual.

That's because we don't just complete the Hero's Journey once and then stop. In writing a better story for yourself, you're going to have to answer the Call to Adventure multiple times. You will need to make YES a huge part of your vocabulary.

The other thing you may experience in this journey is that the thing you think you want—i.e. making more money or meeting Mr. Right—isn't the thing that you actually need. This happened to me over and over, where I'd start writing a story about, say, making more money, but my heart would keep bubbling up a narrative about loving myself more. Turns out, if you don't love yourself very much, you'll flit away the money you do get because you don't believe you're worthy of it. Often, my heart was challenging me to come back to fundamental building blocks of love, joy, gratitude, and forgiveness. My heart showed me what I really *needed* in order to have what I really *wanted*.

No matter what you want to focus on, *Author Your Life* can help you write a better story around it. But since I'm writing a book based on my own experiences and what I learned by writing *Lara's Life*, I've structured this book to help you in the following areas where I saw the most breakthroughs:

- Loving yourself
- Discovering your purpose
- Achieving financial abundance
- Connecting to your body and health

I believe someday there will be more categories and, in that sense, *Lara's Life* is ongoing. I think of the *Lara's Life* as having "chapters," and not being a complete work.

As you start your journey, you too may want to think about writing every day like writing a chapter. As you would with journaling, you can write whatever is on your mind or your heart. The big difference between *Author Your Life* and journaling is that we're using the power of writing to create a better *future* instead of to examine the past or even the present. Both are needed, and you can definitely complement this work with journaling (see more on this in the next chapter section, "Your Current Stories," as well as in Chapter Ten under "The Simple Stuff").

Sometimes, when I sit down to write, I'll give myself a chapter title as an affirmation to help guide me. Here are some of the chapter titles I've created in *Lara's Life*:

Relaxing and Enjoying Life

Grateful for the Work!

In the Fight

Listening to Her Body

Confident in Her Abilities

Savings in Abundance

Enjoying the Everyday

It's Safe!

Dreams Come True!

You don't have to worry about "structuring" your story to perfectly match with the Hero's Journey, or plotting it like you would a novel. Nothing about your book has to be sequential, either. While it might help to think about goals and what you want, you'll ultimately be writing what comes to mind when you do the exercises in this book and put pen to paper. This is because your heart knows exactly what your story needs to be.

For my part, I'm still engaging the Hero's Journey every day. I followed the path you'll read about in this book, and I arrived at a better place, but my journey is far from over. There's always more joy, more fulfillment, more abundance that I can make room for in my life.

Practical Help

When I was gathering input on this book, I crafted a Facebook post asking people to help me understand how they wanted to create a better story for themselves. In part, my post said:

We've followed the rules and we've done The Right Thing our whole lives. We've received good grades in school, and now we have good jobs. We go to church and we volunteer in our communities. We give selflessly to others. AND YET. So many of us are carrying tiny splinters in our hearts that remind us, with every single beat, that something is off. The stories of who we are and who we want to be are not aligned.

Then I asked for feedback on a few questions and, holy crap, the response was overwhelming. You may resonate with some of the people who responded and said they:

- Feel like they have no control over how their life is playing out, that they're on autopilot.
- Want to change, but they don't know how or where to begin.
- Have gifts and talents they're not using, but don't see a way to bring them to light.
- Want to overcome imposter syndrome, where they doubt their accomplishments and are afraid of being seen as a fraud.
- Are hungry for deeper, more meaningful relationships.
- Are tired of living paycheck to paycheck.
- Want to believe the universe is in their favor, and that they can tap into the magic and meaning of human existence.

Do you see yourself in any of these responses? Let me tell you, I was pretty much struggling with all of the above when I started my journey. I was also really frustrated because I would read self-help books that would say things like "love yourself" or "write a better story for yourself," but I had no idea how to do any of that. So many books preach about what's wrong, but don't actually help you fix it.

Which is why this book is intentionally practical. As you read each section and as we go through the Hero's Journey together, I'll give you questions to help you think about what to write as you craft a better story.

Then I will give you guided prompts to help set your stories in motion.

The good news is that you don't have to be a great writer (or even a *good* writer or, heck, even think of yourself as a writer at all) to do any of this. Even if your story is just fragments of thought, bullet points, or simple affirmations, it can still work. One of the most powerful things I ever wrote was "Lara loves herself." Just penning that on a piece of paper started bending the fabric of the universe in my favor.

The one thing that this journey does require is time. I know how hard this can be for so many people, because time is a precious commodity. When people ask us how we are, our answer is, so often, "Busy."

As I'll make clear in the next section, you don't have to spend hours on this every day. I wrote *Lara's Life* nearly every morning for a year, for about 20 minutes every day.

A year might seem like forever when you think about your journey. It did for me, too, when I started out. But I was so desperate to live my life differently, I was willing to spend the time making sure all the big pieces could *thunk* into place. And while the Hero's Journey will always be an ongoing quest for me, it has gotten easier. I've slayed some big demons that were holding me back in fundamental ways. Now they're out of the way, the path is much clearer.

In a quick-fix world, we want to think that change can happen by swallowing a pill or taking a quiz. I wish I could tell you that this process is quick and easy. It's neither of those things, but it's fundamentally doable, and that's the heart of this book: To give you the roadmap to follow so you can write a better story for yourself and start living the life you want.

Your Current Stories

In the *Author Your Life* journey, you're going to put pen to paper and write out all the things that you want to have happen to you. You're going to tell the story you *want* to come true. In the process, the stories you are *already* telling yourself are going to rise up like that Balrog fire monster from *Lord of the Rings*. And that monster is going to fight you, because it likes being there and it doesn't want to go away.

This part is important, so get out your highlighter. **The hardest part of your journey is going to be the tension between your two stories: The one you're telling yourself currently, and the one you want to be true instead. The crux of this whole book rests in that disparity.**

When you find yourself frustrated and in tears because the new story you're writing isn't coming true yet, don't give up. It just means there's an old story that needs erasing. Or maybe revising. It can also mean that things are working, they're changing, but you just can't see them yet.

Today, as I write this, my new stories are working. They are locked and loaded, and my life is markedly different. To that end, my biggest changes have been on the inside. My mind is quieted. My heart is softened. I feel filled up with love. And it's these changes on the *inside* that have led to everything being different on the *outside*.

The good news is that you can also try lots of additional tactics to change your life story. I'm giving you resources at the end of this book because, in my journey, I read tons of self-help, listened to about a bazillion podcasts, watched videos, made vision boards—you name it, I did it. This book might not be exactly what you need, and that's okay. One resource rarely is. I recommend trying a bunch of different things to find what works for you.

In the *Author Your Life* journey, when you put pen to paper, you're not trying to re-write the stories of the past. If you were hurt by someone when you were eight years old, you're not going to write a story in which you suddenly weren't hurt. That hurt might still exist, so we don't want to dismiss or negate it.

Our past may surface in this process, and that's great. That's a powerful part of *Author Your Life*. The goal is to accept those things and fold them into a better future, not try to pretend they never happened.

Some people may ask you: What is your story? Instead, I'm asking: What do you want your story to be? Some of self-help gurus will say: Change your story. I'm saying instead: Here's how.

That's the heart of *Author Your Life*. And if you're ready to be the hero in the story of your life, keep reading.

TWO

Answering the Call

The first part of the Hero's Journey is the Call to Adventure. That phrase can be a little tricky, because the word "adventure" implies that we're jumping right into the part of the story where things really get going. Frodo and Sam leave the Shire! Dorothy is wind-swept into Oz! Neo is given the choice between the red and blue pills!

But before any of that happens—before the tension starts to ratchet up in a story—there's a sort of...*itchiness* in the main character's life. There's an uneasy sense that something is off. The character just doesn't fit in (Harry Potter feeling out of place with the Dursleys), or they're wondering about the limits of their current situation (Belle feeling constrained by her village in *Beauty and the Beast*).

The restlessness? *That's the call.*

I'm going to guess that if you're reading this book, you're experiencing some itchiness in your life. The feeling that you have right now that something could be different or better—well, that's the start of *everything*.

And yes, I can see you over there with your hand in the air, waving furiously. I know what you're going to ask: "Are you sure there is a Call to Adventure for me and my life?"

And the answer is: *Oh, honey, is there ever.*

You were put on this planet to do something that is uniquely, awesomely, inherently *you*. If you don't know what that something is, don't panic! We're going to take a deep dive into finding your purpose later in this book. I've got your back on this, I swear. For right now, your only job is to just take a breath and get low-down raw and real with the fact that you believe there could be something *more* for you. We don't have to know what *more* is yet. We don't have to define it. We just have to stop and say, "Yep, it's there."

Because, in spite of its name, the Call to Adventure does not mean you suddenly *start having adventures*. I'd argue that in most cases, it's the opposite. The Call to Adventure is a call to pipe down and listen to what your truest, highest self is actually saying to you.

The answer could be adventures! That's totally cool. But transformation doesn't happen just because you pack up everything you own and get on a plane to Italy. I mean, Elizabeth Gilbert's journey started well before she crossed an ocean in her bestselling memoir, *Eat, Pray, Love*. I'd argue that her journey really started when she found herself sobbing on the cold bathroom tile wondering why she was miserable.

Answering the Call to Adventure is simply the willingness to say, "Yes, I'll listen." You're listening to yourself and to your heart. You're quieting your mind and getting still as you do.

This critical stillness happens *throughout* the Hero's Journey. You say yes at the beginning. And yes again after you start. And yes again when things get hard. And yes again and yes again and yes again. Not yes to *others*, but yes to your own heart—every step along the way.

I Have Become Comfortably Numb

In our culture, we're really, really good at ignoring the Call to Adventure. We fill our lives with everything *except* the work to align ourselves with what will make us happiest. I've talked to many people who perhaps had an inkling that there was a Call to Adventure they weren't listening to, but the idea of actually answering it was overwhelming—both because of what it would require, and how comfortably "okay" they were at present.

When I started my own Hero's Journey, I knew I wanted a better life in many ways, but I didn't realize how bad things had gotten. Only when I put pen to paper and really listened to my heart did my eyes open to the yawning chasm between how I wanted my life to be, and the truth of how it actually was.

It's so easy to think things are fine, just fine. I mean, after all, when I started my Hero's Journey, I didn't have any major health issues. My husband Rob and I had insurance, and our living space was secure—

meaning we didn't think the bank was going to come take our house at any minute, or that the government was going to round us up and kick us out of the place we called home. I was employed, and Rob, while not making much, was also employed running his own local ice cream business.

So all that right there? It's huge. It's more than a lot of people have, and it can be hard sometimes to balance gratitude for all the things you have (including white privilege in my case), with the fact that you *know* that things are missing.

It can also be hard to admit that we are allowing ourselves to sink into numbing behaviors when we're mostly doing okay. For those of us who pay our bills on time, go to work, and try to be good people, it can be hard to admit that we're still trying to turn down the dial on our lives in order to tune out the Call to Adventure. It's everything from having too much wine at night to bingeing on the *Great British Baking Show* to endlessly scrolling on Facebook for hours. (If you're me, check all the above!)

I know I'm not alone in this. For instance, in one of my surveys, I got this response from a busy mom:

Do I even want a better story for myself? Do I need one? It sounds like a lot of work, and how much payoff will there be? Is it inertia? Is it that I'm comfortable in the place I'm at? Maybe a weird hybrid of those two things? When it's the end of the day, and I'm tired from work and parenting and not understanding why the dog can't do numbers one and two on a single trip outside, I will need to feel particularly inspired to Answer the Call rather than bingeing on The Good Place.

I totally get it. Answering the Call is extraordinarily hard, because our lives are so filled to the brim with other stuff. Like taking kids to soccer and an endless to-do list. Or tons of drama, where we go from one crisis to another, making it impossible to stop and take a breath and get honest about how life is really going. We might even be caught in a cycle blaming others, believing that *someone else* is keeping us from a better story.

Whatever is keeping you from listening to the Call to Adventure, the first step is acknowledging that no one is responsible for your story but you, and that your journey can't start until you begin to carve out tiny pockets of stillness in your life. (More on exactly *how* to do that at the end of this chapter.)

Only You Can Answer Your Call to Adventure

In her bestselling book *You Are A Badass*, Jen Sincero talks about the importance of writing your own story:

"You're the author of your own life—not your parents, not your society, not your partner, not your friends, not the bullies who called you Fatzilla in junior high—and the sooner you decide to write yourself a better script, the sooner you get to live a more awesome life."

Jen may have been speaking metaphorically about writing a better script for yourself, but in this book, I am *very literally* suggesting you write a better script.

Yet it can be daunting to come to terms with the idea that we, and we alone, are in charge of our stories and that we are the ones who have to put pen to paper to make all these revisions. I can't tell you how many years I spent with a sharp sliver of anger lodged in my heart for things that happened to me growing up, and how I thought that the people who had hurt me were responsible for removing the anger and healing the wound.

Eventually, I realized that in order to really Answer the Call, I couldn't wait until the wrongs against me were righted, because they might never be. If I waited for everything to work itself out before I told my heart it was okay to stop being bitter, my heart was going to shrivel up and disappear before that ever happened.

I'd still be waiting if that were the case. For ex-boyfriends to apologize. For former bosses to realize they'd been complete jerkfaces. For my husband to walk the dog and do the dishes as regularly as I think he should.

Spoiler alert: *Those things are never going to happen.*

So I can either be miserable in my head about the fact that my reality isn't matching up with how I *think* things should be going, or I can decide to write a new story, where my heart is full and happy, and I have joy and peace in my life every day.

Right now, you might be angry at the story you were served up on a cold plate of *this sucks*. Maybe your partner left you. Maybe you just got laid off. Maybe you have suffered physical or emotional abuse. Maybe [insert a thousand million hurtful options here].

The question is not whether these things happened and affected you. The question is whether you're ignoring the Call to Adventure because you're hoping that someone *else* will come along and change your story for you, because what happened to you wasn't fair, and it wasn't right.

Alas, you can wait by the window or the computer or the front door all day and all night for the rest of your life, but no one is coming to change your story for you. There's not a friend, nor a true love, nor even a therapist who can do that. Sure, those folks I just listed can help. But at the end of the day, fixing your story is on you.

There is admittedly some sadness in this, because man, wouldn't it be nice if our story were someone else's problem, and by *forcing other people to act differently* we could be happier?

The truth is, of course, that no one's actions will make us happier if we're dependent on them. If we say, *I can only Answer the Call when X person does Y*, then the fight is already over. We've already lost, because we're giving away all our power to someone else. They're in control of the narrative, not us.

Instead, true power is in taking control of your own destiny and deciding that you don't have to wait until someone else gets your story right—because you're the one writing it.

You Can Answer the Call to Adventure Now

Just so we're clear, you get to answer your Call to Adventure right now, exactly as you are. If part of you is thinking you'll do it when the kids are out of school or when you lose 30 pounds, please know, you don't need to put restrictions on this. You don't have to be perfect. You don't have to earn a better income or drive a nicer car.

At its core, Answering the Call simply means saying yes to living the story that's in your heart—without worrying about how it's going to shake out. What will it mean? How will it look when you say yes? You can leave that to the universe.

All you have to do is say yes to your story right now.

How to Answer the Call to Adventure

Answering the Call to Adventure is all about listening and not doing.

Instead of saying, "I'm going to get my ass in gear and finish all those craft projects!" it's pausing and thinking, "I'm going to connect to my heart. I'm going to get comfortable with what my truest, highest self is saying. I'm going to listen."

When you do that, you might be surprised. The answer might not even include craft projects.

Because of this, answering the Call to Adventure can happen anywhere. I answered the Call to Adventure at my kitchen table every morning at 4:00 a.m. for months on end. I wrote in notebooks. I read books. I meditated. I was doing huge, transformational work with enormous ripple effects. And I did it before dawn in an old, creaky chair wearing yoga pants and slippers. To Answer the Call, don't think you have to pack up and leave your spouse, quit your job, or say adios to your kids.

You can Answer the Call on the bus on the way to work.

You can Answer the Call waiting in the parking lot to pick up your kid after school

You can Answer the Call in the sliver of time you have before you head to bed.

When I started this process, I had no idea about the things I was going to have to face, or the wounds I would need to heal in my life. I just had an itchiness. And I simply said, "Yes, I'll sit with this feeling and see where it takes me." That was how I Answered the Call.

Here are some ways you can begin to Answer the Call today.

Exercise #1: Make Time for Stillness

This is where it all starts. I'm asking you to give yourself 20 minutes three times each week. That's one hour out of the 168 hours that are in each week, or .595 percent. No matter how busy your schedule is or what the demands are on you, you deserve to take .595 percent of your time to Answer the Call on your life.

Take a few moments right now to think about where, when, and how you can take that time. Is it in the mornings, before everyone gets up? I am an early bird, so the ass-crack of dawn works for me, but I understand not everyone's biorhythms are the same. You don't have to choose the same time every day, but I will say there is enormous value in creating a routine.

Designing a pattern makes it more likely that we will remember to do something, and thus repeat it. If you need to, schedule your time for stillness. Make slowing down and getting quiet part of your day, just like you would attending a meeting or picking up the dry cleaning.

Ideally, your time for stillness will be interruption-free. So it's less important where you do it, and more that it meets the following criteria:

- You can sit down
- You can take deep breaths
- You can pull out a notebook
- You can close your eyes

You can do all those things on a subway or in your office with the door closed, so I'm not particular about the place. But it might not hurt take a few moments now to think about where you might be able to plug into stillness three times each week. If you've gotten this far in this book, I know you can do it.

If you need extra help figuring out where you can get .595 percent of your time back, I'd recommend picking up a time management book like *I Know How She Does It* by Laura Vanderkam. Chances are, you *have* the time, you just need a little help figuring out where it's hiding.

Exercise #2: Get a Notebook and Pen

I like to go old school on this process, and the

research backs me up. When we take the time to write something out, our brain has more time to digest the information. It sticks more.

It's not a deal-breaker, so if you need to use a laptop to write out your stories, go for it (and we'll get started on the actual writing part in the next chapter). But getting away from screens is a good thing to practice in general. If you're away from your computer, it reduces the likelihood that you'll be checking email or looking at social media.

This is going to be your book. This is where your story is going to go. Your notebook doesn't have to be fancy, but it will have power. Keep it close, and get ready to fill it up!

Exercise #3: Get Comfy With Challenges

The protagonist in any journey has to say yes to challenges; that's just how this whole thing goes. And challenges, when we accept them, lead to change. I wish there were an easier way to get you from Point A to Point B in the story of your life, but this process is set. It's as immovable law as the law of gravity: You can wish it didn't work this way, but your face hitting the pavement is going to say otherwise every time.

Many of us see challenges as a bad thing, so it can take time to accept that this is a powerful part of the process. Looking back, I know that when I hit road-blocks in my journey—like a financial setback or a huge fight with Rob—I kept thinking something was going wrong. Now, I understand that everything that comes into my life can be used for my greatest good, even the challenging stuff. *Especially* the challenging stuff.

It can be counterintuitive to think about it this way, but challenges can be used to refine us and help us. You don't get to be a diamond without a lot of pressure on a hunk of coal first.

At the start of every journey, the hero thinks they want one thing, but by the end of the tale, the hero realizes they actually want something else entirely. In the first *Thor* movie, for example, our favorite blond demigod starts out wanting to avenge an act of war against his people. By the end of the movie, his goal is to protect people from war whenever possible and to rule as a wise king.

Author Your Life isn't a genie that gives you exactly what you want when you write a story about it. The power is not in the getting, but in the creating—in the writing and the engagement of the story. The universe will help it be the story we need it to be.

I recently heard a *SuperSoul* Conversation, where Oprah interviewed poet Mark Nepo, who summed it up beautifully in this quote: "Asking for what we need doesn't always lead to getting what we need. But the reward for asking for what we need is that we become intimate with our own nature. We learn who we are."

When challenges arise, don't freak out. It actually means you're on the right path. If you weren't experiencing hurdles, you wouldn't be on the adventure.

Exercise #4: Fill out this Permission Slip

Many years ago, when I was working a full-time job at the University of Michigan and publishing books on the side, I kept waiting for the moment when I could change my schedule so I could devote more time to novels. I kept waiting for someone—my boss, my husband, my agent, the mailman—to tell me to go for it. No one ever did. It was up to me to give myself the green light to live the life I wanted to live.

As a Midwesterner and a rule-follower, I *still* seek permission in just about every situation. The difference is that now I know I can give it to myself. I talk to myself regularly and grant myself the power to do what I need to do.

I don't use the word power lightly here. In fact, let's put it in all-caps and spell it like the badass word it is, shall we? POWAAAHHH.

And guess what? I'm passing that power on to you.

I give you permission to give yourself permission.

I want you to fill out this permission slip and, if you can, display it somewhere you can see it regularly.

I [Your Name] have permission to answer the Call to Adventure in my life. I have permission to take at least .595 percent of my time each week for myself. I can write a better story for myself, and I have permission to do exactly that starting today.

Signed, [Your Name][Date]

THREE

The Leap of Faith

In the stories we love, the protagonist starts out on a quest without knowing exactly what's in front of them. In the holiday movie *Elf*, Buddy heads off to New York City in search of his real dad without any inkling that he'll fall in love, make friends, make mistakes, get a job, get yelled at repeatedly, and ultimately wind up saving Christmas.

Because the Leap of Faith requires…well, *faith*, we have to trust that everything that is happening to us is part of the story. Like Buddy, we don't always get to decide what the adventure looks like. We just have to continually trust that if we're actively writing out our stories, the universe is listening and helping us get to our heart's desire.

Right now, we're all sharing the same Leap of Faith: that writing down the story of how we want our lives to be can help us *live those lives*. Now, your story might have you connecting with your kids more and my story might be all about becoming a champion figure skater, and that's a-okay. The process works no matter what your story is about or what details you're putting on paper.

That said, there are four areas where I want to help you take the Leap of Faith and write a better story, because it's where I struggled the most and it's where I know other people have trouble, too. I listed these areas earlier in the book, but it's worth repeating, because it's how we're organizing the Leap of Faith section:

- Loving yourself
- Discovering your purpose
- Achieving financial abundance
- Connecting to your body and health

These will be the areas we'll focus on, but that's not to say you can't write a story about parenting, travel, cooking—whatever you want. Once you understand how to put all this into practice, you can apply the work to any area of your life you wish.

Evidence: It's What's for Dinner

I know all of this can seem super woo-woo and unbelievable. Like, sure, it's called a Leap of Faith, but can you really just write your life like a novel and then watch it come true?

Obviously, I believe the answer is yes because, hello there, I'm Lara and I'm writing this book *right now*.

But more than that, there's evidence that underscores the life-changing force of what we're doing here.

Dr. James Pennebaker from the University of Texas at Austin has studied the connections between writing and healing for years. He uses "writing therapy" to help people deal with psychological trauma, and his research shows that writing can boost immune system function, making people physically healthier. Writing or "storifying" experiences helps people approach what's happened to them more objectively and can ultimately provide perspective on and understanding of these experiences.

It's for this reason that we're going to write our stories in the third person, like we're characters in a novel. So instead of writing "I have a great relationship with my husband," you're going to write it like you're observing yourself as a character: "Ashley has a great relationship with her husband."

Michigan State University and the University of Michigan published a study in *Scientific Reports* in 2017 that said talking to yourself in the third person can help you psychologically, even helping you control stressful situations. "Essentially, we think referring to yourself in the third person leads people to think about themselves more similar to how they think about others," said Jason Moser, an associate professor of psychology at Michigan State University, who helped lead the study.

This matters because we are often *so* super mean to ourselves, berating and beating ourselves up in ways we would never treat another person. Raise your hand if you are usually way nicer to others than you are to yourself. And yes, I see all those hands out there! Mine is one of them.

31

Writing in 3rd person instead of 1st

Alternatively, if we try writing out situations like we're a character in a book, it can fool our brain and our emotions into believing the narrative a bit more. Which means that instead of writing out "I'm nice to my co-worker, Becky," (which your brain is already calling bullshit on because, let's be honest, Becky bugs the living crap out of you), it might be more useful to write it in the third person like a story: "Lara smiles at Becky, and engages her in conversation. She connects with what Becky has to say. She listens and empathizes. When things are challenging at work, she is able to find solutions readily and is not quick to blame others, including Becky." Our brains are more likely to go along with this version than the first-person version.

Because Physics

It's not just the social sciences but the physical sciences that may also hold clues about why *Author Your Life* can work.

In quantum mechanics, which is the branch of physics that studies the tiniest building blocks of the universe like atoms and quarks, scientists have tried to measure the physical characteristics of subatomic particles, such as position or momentum, but haven't been able to pin them down.

"A particle simply does not have a precise position before measurement, any more than the ripples of a pond do," says David J. Griffiths in *Introduction to Quantum Mechanics, Second Edition* (Pearson Education,

2005). In other words, scientists theorize that behavior can be influenced by observation.

If scientists may be able to influence how particles behave just by observing them, imagine the influence we can have when we direct energy or thought (or words!) toward not just a particle but our entire lives. If reality is perception, then all we have to do is change the story of what we're perceiving.

Faith in the Power of Words

It's a beautiful and powerful thing to believe that writing your future can actually *change your future*. Look at what has manifested because J.K. Rowling gave us Harry Potter, and that was fiction. She wasn't even *trying* to make Hogwarts real but, today, the whole Harry Potter world isn't in our imaginations anymore because there is literally a magical place at Universal Studios in Florida where you can drink butterbeer, get sorted into your house, talk to Hagrid, and buy the exact right wand for you. Heck, you don't even have to go very far to see and touch Harry's world—you can buy your own owl at Target and get a time-turning necklace online.

That was something made-up, something fantastical that was never intended to be literal, so imagine what you can manifest if you're actually, you know, trying!

Even the Bible says that the world began with the power of words. "In the beginning was the Word, and the Word was with God and the Word was God" (John 1:1).

In June 2018, five journalists in Maryland's *Capital Gazette* newsroom were killed by a terrorist. Gunned down in cold blood and for what? Their words. There is a reason dictators and corrupt leaders target the free press when they take over—because words and stories have power, and that power can be threatening.

Author Amy Ferris had an incredible Facebook post in 2018 about the slaying of the five journalists titled "What I Know," and here, in part, is what she said (reprinted here with permission):

"Words matter. Words change lives. Words inspire hope. Words can infuriate and annihilate and they can break your heart. Words can also lift you, support you, make you feel heart full. Words, how we use them, how we say them, how we write them. A story written can ignite a dormant passion, can awaken a mission, can encourage a next step, can change the direction of your life."

Once More, With Feeling

In many of the Leap of Faith sections, I'm also going to ask you to stop and feel your feelings. Because writing is great—it's huge and it can be life-changing—but often the power of transformation requires that you begin to actually *feel* the change, too. In her book *Lucky Bitch*, Denise Duffield-Thomas puts it this way:

"Thinking is not enough to manifest what you want. You have to *feel* it. You have to get into that space of living it before it actually shows up in the real world. Every cell of your being has to be convinced."

That means that in the Leap of Faith sections, I'm going to encourage you to put down the pen and get comfy with your emotions. So let's say you write something like, "[Your Name] has happiness and peace throughout the day."

Super simple, right? Then, I might encourage you to close your eyes and feel yourself having happiness and peace throughout the day. Create the feeling if you have to, *make* it be there if you must—and then picture yourself in all aspects of your day with that feeling. At your desk at work—peace. At the grocery store with people crashing their carts into you—peace. Driving in rush-hour traffic—peace. And let that peace wash over you.

Tapping into these feelings is transformational. And this right here is a plug for you to develop a regular mediation practice if you don't have one. Like you, I've read all the articles and books that say how good meditation can be. But to me, before I actually started doing it, meditation was like drinking green tea—something that probably was decent for you, but it wasn't going to make a huge difference overall.

Turns out, meditation changed everything. There are a ton of easy-to-use apps available that can help you begin to meditate. I like the Insight Timer, which offers guided meditations. That means I don't have to sit there and try to empty my brain and keep thoughts from ping-ponging around in my head. Instead, I have an expert who's leading me where I need to go, gently and safely. These meditations help me focus, help me feel, help me heal. It doesn't have to take long; I meditate for around 10 minutes each day. That's it!

If this sounds terrifying and you're like, *Shut up this book was supposed to be about writing, not about feeling, I want my money back*, I totally get how scary this can be. Feeling much of anything was a big shift for me. I grew up in a family that didn't really acknowledge feelings, and we certainly didn't talk about them. When I did tell my parents about my feelings, they often told me to feel differently. Whether it was about a career path ("You don't want to be an archaeologist, they don't make any money") or my older brother hitting me ("He's not hurting you, he's just teasing, don't let him bother you"), I was frequently told it wasn't okay to have the feelings that I did. I should have different ones.

I learned quickly that feelings were not my friend. They were a liability. I shoved them down and covered them with a thick blanket of *it's fine*. I remember going through a tough time in college and thinking, "My feelings aren't real. They don't matter. They don't exist." I really thought that by not acknowledging them, they would just go away.

Spoiler alert: They don't go away. They just find different ways to seep out.

For me, they seeped out when I reached for that fourth glass of wine. They seeped out when I didn't feel I deserved money so I spent it until my bank balance read zero. They seeped out when I pushed people away and hid from the world.

So yes, I get that feeling stuff is exceptionally hard. Feelings are scary. They can be painful. Shit, I used to say to my therapist that the whole goal of me sitting with her was just to get me to feel my feelings. I was joking, half shrugging it off, but she didn't exactly chuckle because that was precisely the crux of what I needed to do.

In writing, we're often told to embody our characters. This means to a large degree feeling what they feel. Our stories can't exist if we don't connect what we're writing with what we're feeling.

How to Take the Leap of Faith

When I first began writing *Lara's Life*, it was pretty bare bones: *Lara has peace. Lara has abundance.*

I was trying to just get my bearings and figure out what in the world I was doing. But, gradually, the author in me started really setting the scene and painting a picture.

Even when I was flat broke, I wrote about how it felt to pay all my bills with ease, and the delight I experienced when I opened my bank statement and there was more than enough there. Even when I wanted to pull away from everyone and everything around me, I wrote how I was comfortable with vulnerability, how safe and loved I felt with Rob, and how at ease and joyful I was when we had sex.

The point wasn't that I wrote things in flowery sentences and every line was perfect. You don't have to be a great writer for this process to work. It doesn't matter if you make lists with bullet points or simply write out affirmations. What matters is that you imagine a better story and you put that story on paper in some way that works for you.

Of course, I'm here to help, and we'll get into the details of how to take the Leap of Faith in the four specific areas I outlined earlier. For now, though, we're going to take some time to think about the big picture: What do you want to think, feel, and have as you begin to author your life?

From the last chapter: Get out your notebook and pen and find a quiet space. Ideally you're giving yourself 20 minutes three days each week in said quiet space. But if all you have is five minutes in a single stretch—or two!—do what you can with the exercises throughout the book. You'd be amazed at the progress you can make in two minutes.

Now, here we go.

Exercise #1: Think of yourself as a novelist creating a character who gets to have the life they've always dreamed of. That character is you, of course, but you're going to think of them in the third person. Write down the details of what this character has and does. Where does this character travel? What kind of relationships do they have? What does a fulfilling life look like for them? Don't worry about writing a story around what comes to your mind in these areas; just jot down the big ideas.

Exercise #2: Now that you have a sense of what a fulfilling life looks like for your character, flesh out some of those details:

- How do they feel?
- Who are they with?
- What thoughts do they have?
- What do they see?
- How do they treat the people around them?
- What do they know to be true?

Your heart knows the answers to all these questions. You don't have to over-think anything. For now, just put pen to paper and see what comes up.

Exercise #3: Give your book a title. What do you want your story to be called? I love having my name in the title, because it reminds me that this is my story and I get to make it whatever I want it to be. Get a Sharpie and scrawl your title on the front of that new notebook of yours. Need ideas? Here are a few:

- *Elena Kicks Ass!*
- *Happier Heather*
- *Anna Saves the Planet and Herself*
- *The Ultimate Liz*

Or, you can be like my friend Marnie, who gave herself the most kick-butt title of all time: *Dancing in the Kitchen: Marnie's Recipes for Living Joyfully (Even When Your Apron is on Fire)*.

FOUR

Loving Yourself

This chapter focuses on how to do battle with the voice inside your head that continually tells you that you're not good enough, that you shouldn't try anything new, that you're fundamentally flawed, that no one really likes you…on and on. Does this voice sound familiar?

I call this my inner garbage person. I stole that term from a podcast that I really love called *By the Book*, on which two really smart, funny women read a self-help book and then, for two weeks, do what the book says to see if it works.

One of the hosts, Jolenta Greenberg, actually called herself a garbage person during the podcast. She was sort of joking but not really joking. Meaning this super cool, funny woman who has a nationally broadcast podcast really thought, at the end of the day, that she sucked. That she was a terrible person. And I was like, *Holy crap, I think I'm a garbage person, too*! I could hear my own beliefs reflected back to me in her words.

The thing about believing you're a garbage person is

that it's not as if you go around flogging yourself and wailing, "I'm a garbage person." The belief is a lot sneakier and hides in crafty places so you don't always recognize it.

My garbage person loved to hide behind perfection, for example. It made sure I put aaalll the pressure on myself to be exactly right, so that no one would know the truth about how I felt about myself.

For example, I'd do a great presentation at work, but instead of feeling good about what had gone right, I'd hyper-focus on the comment someone made afterward about one of the slides being hard to read. I would panic. One flaw in one slide meant I had *failed*. The truth was out: I was a worthless colleague and everyone knew it.

Or when I had a day off and time to do exactly what I wanted, I would find myself in full-on tears, or worse, irritable and unhappy. My inner garbage person was freaking out, because garbage people don't *get* time off to be happy and do what they want. Deep down, I'd feel like everything I did that was good was a fluke, because I was constantly on the verge of being unmasked as a total loser.

Cue the eating and the drinking to make those thoughts go away.

Cue the retreating into myself and pushing Rob away.

Cue the hiding from friends to make social interactions disappear.

All the difficult things that were manifesting in my life (financial struggles, a heavier weight, too much drinking, no sex life, etc.) were manifestations of my inner garbage person.

That's why I put loving yourself front and center in this book because it's so foundational to writing a better story. If we can't figure out how to love ourselves, the rest of our journey is doomed.

Loving Yourself is the Key to Everything Else

One of the areas where I've struggled the most in *Author Your Life* (and in life in general) is with my finances. I have always been challenged with managing a budget, not over-spending, and generally being smart with money. I'll go into this in greater detail in the financial abundance section, but trust me when I tell you that my relationship with money has, historically, been pretty messed up.

When I started *Author Your Life*, I figured that the answer to my problems was of course *more money*. If I could just make more, I'd be fine. Natch!

So at the start of my journey, I was hell-bent on making that money. I wrote about how much I wanted to earn, I hired a life coach, I networked and kicked open doors of opportunity, and I said yes to every gig that came my way, just to get a paycheck.

I started *Author Your Life* in January, and by May, I was making more than I had made in my life—ever. Sounds great, right?

The only problem is that my garbage person didn't know what to *do* with all that money. It felt so strange to have it. I didn't think I deserved it. I wasn't truly grateful for it because, deep down, I thought it was a fluke. After all, garbage people don't have abundance. They don't deserve success or wealth, and it makes them so uncomfortable that they spend it away. So that's what I did. As soon as that money came in, it was gone.

This revealed such an important lesson for me: We can't accept the better story that the universe sends us if we don't do battle with our inner garbage person. We can't get to our happy ending if we don't slay this dragon.

You might be fine financially, but maybe there are other areas of your life where your feelings of self-suck manifest. For instance, I know someone who has been trying to find a job for almost two years now. This person is smart, funny, talented—they'd be a great asset to any team. I know their résumé is good because they keep getting interviews, but they can't stick the landing. I would bet you there's a garbage person in them somewhere sabotaging their success, constantly whispering, "Who am I to deserve a great new gig? The truth is, I don't, so I should probably just stay here in this crap job."

Whether it's more money or a better job or meeting Mr. Right or finding your dream house or not putting crap into your body, it all starts with loving yourself.

The good news is that in the process of writing *Lara's Life*, I really did learn to love myself. I literally buried my garbage person in the back yard in a ceremony. I wrote on a piece of paper all the things that my garbage person said about me, then I tore that paper into shreds, dumped it into a bowl, lit the paper on fire, and buried the ashes. I did this all while on my knees, thanking my garbage person for trying to protect me and help me, but telling it that it wasn't in charge any more. Honestly, the whole thing probably had my neighbors scratching their heads in bewilderment. But I did it.

That's not to say that I never struggle with self-esteem or that my garbage person doesn't try to crawl out of its grave, zombie-style, and whisper its lies in my ear. I'm still living my story—and I always will be. Remember the part where you have to answer the call not just once but again and again? Our journey requires that we continually say yes to the universe over and over. Yes, I'll keep learning. Yes, I'll keep refining. Yes, I'll keep going.

Loving Yourself Unleashes Compassion, Joy, and Forgiveness

Compassion, joy, and forgiveness are three things that we hear a lot about in self-help books and at church and in any kind of spiritual growth program. It turns out that all three flow directly from loving ourselves.

I suppose it sounds counter-intuitive in a way—certainly there's a school of belief that says loving ourselves will turn us into selfish, self-absorbed monsters. But the *opposite* is true. We loathe in others what we loathe in ourselves; and we love in others what we've learned to love in ourselves.

In my case, I've discovered that if I'm really annoyed by someone, it's because they're showing me a part of myself that I don't like. Let's take know-it-alls as an example. This personality type pushes my buttons like no other. I want to run screaming from them. Know-it-alls are the *worst*.

I'm laughing as I write this, because I'm literally sitting here writing a how-to book. It takes a very specific type of personality to say, "I know soooo much about something that I'm going to tell you how to do it." Do you see how close that is to a know-it-all? It's certainly a fine line, and one I've definitely crossed before. That's because saying three little words—"I don't know"—used to be very hard for me. I grew up with know-it-alls everywhere around me, and having the answer, *any* answer, became a default part of my personality.

It's only in recent years that I've learned the value in embracing "I don't know." I'm lucky that I've had good bosses and an amazing husband who model this for me. They make it okay to prioritize being curious over being right, and to value discovery. And because I've chosen to love myself, I can exercise compassion when I exhibit know-it-all tendencies. I am quicker to forgive myself instead of beating myself up. I can understand the bigger picture of where this behavior comes from (hello, childhood!) and send loving feelings to the little girl who became a know-it-all just to fit in and survive.

When people rip each other apart with shame and condemnation, what they're really reacting to is a part of themselves that they haven't learned to love. It goes from individuals to families to communities, all the way up to a national and global scale.

Think about all the politicians who have railed against gay rights and the gay community, only to be discovered as harboring a secret gay identity. Because they hated a part of themselves and feared it, they heaped that hate on others.

Online trolls? They are hurting others because they themselves hurt.

Your nasty neighbor? They're only angry at you because, deep down, they're angry at themselves.

When we hate ourselves, we hate others. In contrast, when we love ourselves, we can love others, and our capacity for compassion increases. We can understand others more easily. We can treat others with more respect and kindness, because we're treating ourselves with more respect and kindness. We can forgive others, because we have forgiven ourselves.

When I started loving myself, I became more joyful. My heart was less bitter. These were things I wanted so badly, because I could feel the anger and fury at the state of the world eating away at me. American politics was filling my soul with so much poison that I could taste it in the back of my throat.

I could see the political anger taking down close friends, who were becoming rage monsters, building walls, screaming into the void, and destroying themselves in the process.

I realized that in order to be the most effective in the fight for the values and beliefs I had, I couldn't meet angry hate with angry hate. I couldn't wait for major political wrongs to be righted until I told my heart it was okay to stop being bitter.

So I started by loving myself, and as a result, my lens on the world became brighter, more full of hope and joy. I discovered I could address issues and fight for what I believed in without being overwhelmed by anger. My heart was fuller and happier. Loving myself changed everything, and I believe it can change everything for you, too.

How to Slay Your Inner Garbage Person and Love Yourself

Exercise #1: Write that You Love Yourself

Every day, I want one line in your book to be: [Your Name] loves herself.

You can write it more than once. That's great! But at least once is essential.

This is where it all started for me. I didn't know what else to do when I began this journey. I knew loving myself was important, but I didn't know how to change the fact that, deep down, I really sort of hated myself. So I started here. I just wrote down that I loved myself. And slowly, gradually, I began to believe it. After a time, it came true.

If you take nothing else from this book, take this one exercise. Do this. Write down that you love yourself. It's the most powerful part of your story.

Exercise #2: Ask yourself what someone who loves

47

herself *does.*

When I hated myself, it was easy to drink too much and spend away all my money and stuff carbs into my face like there was no tomorrow. But when I started writing about how much I loved myself, I simultaneously began to write about how a person who loves themselves *behaves.*

For instance, I began to create a story for Lara where she loved her body and treated it respectfully. (That didn't mean that I loved my body and began treating it respectfully right away. But this was definitely the first step.) I created a story where I was compassionate with myself, showing myself kindness instead of beating myself up all the darn time. Here are examples of things I wrote, straight from *Lara's Life*:

- Lara loves her body and appreciates how strong it is. When she looks at herself in the mirror, she is filled up with gratitude and sees beauty and power.
- Lara treats herself with compassion and kindness. When things go wrong or she makes a mistake, she shows herself the same compassion she would show Rob or a close friend. She puts her hand on her heart and feels love for herself.
- Lara fuels her body with healthy food. She makes good choices for herself because she loves herself. Healthy food draws her like a magnet. She listens to her body and feeds it what it truly wants.

I know this is simple text, and it's not like I was writing a Pulitzer Prize-winning book here. But there is power in simplicity and in writing down what you want. Please don't feel like you have to write the world's greatest story. Instead, start by asking yourself what thoughts and actions occur when you love yourself. What do you do on a daily basis? What thoughts do you have? How do you treat yourself and others? Then, begin to write them down in the third person, like a character who is already doing them.

HOW DOES IT FEEL?

Exercise #3: Do the Small Things

Slowly, I began to give myself permission to love myself in very small ways, every day.

It started with taking off my makeup at night. I always went to bed with my mascara, eyeliner, eye shadow, and foundation still in place, and woke up every morning looking like an over-the-hill drag queen. It was decidedly *not* pretty. So at night, I started washing my face.

I'd like to tell you that this was easy, but even this small thing was a fight. I didn't want to. *What was the big deal?* I'd wonder. *So what if I just left it on?* Intellectually, I knew it was better for my skin and my body if I cleaned my face at night. But it was hard to be bothered to do it. Taking care of myself in this way didn't feel natural at all. Loving myself enough to give myself clean, healthy skin wasn't something that seemed right.

Nevertheless, I did it night after night—often forcing myself to go through the motions.

Same with flossing. I've loathed it my whole life, and I've endured the guilt from my dentist about it for years. Then one day, after writing for a few months that I loved myself, I decided that flossing was another small act of kindness I could show myself. So I folded that into my daily routine, too.

Those were two small things that I decided to do to show myself love. Some others included making an appointment for a mammogram and buying tickets to a show for Rob and I to see together.

Now, it's your turn. Ask yourself: **What small things can you do show yourself a bit of love?** Maybe it's making that doctor's appointment you've been putting off. It could be allowing yourself to get another hour of sleep each night or buying yourself some new clothes, or a fabulous piece of jewelry. Exercise is a big need for many of us, but instead of worrying about starting a full-on exercise regimen, ask yourself if there are ways to simply take a 10-minute walk a few days a week, or do some yoga stretches in your living room.

If you need help keeping these actions top of mind, write them into your story. They can be simple affirmations, such as "Lara flosses at night because she values her body and takes care of it."

Tiny adjustments can have a huge impact. More importantly, these are active demonstrations that you love yourself. Even if they're small, they make an enormous difference.

. . .

Exercise #4: Feel that You Love Yourself

In the previous chapter, I talked about how writing and feeling go hand in hand. Putting your new story down on paper is all well and good, but you also have to feel the emotion of your "character," who is you.

You might have to fake it at first, and that's okay. "Fake it 'til you make it" is totally acceptable—and even necessary. It's not like most of us wake up every day experiencing enormous love for ourselves. It's usually the opposite: The minute we open our eyes and roll out of bed, it's like we're already running behind and generating feelings of "not enough" in ourselves as a result.

So after you write out "[Your Name] loves herself," I want you to put your hand on your heart and close your eyes. Take some deep breaths, and feel that love for yourself. Force it if you have to. Eventually, you won't have to force it; it will just be there naturally. Say out loud, "I love myself," and let your heart fill up with that emotion.

This works with any feeling you want to cultivate, so you can practice it with gratitude, compassion, joy—anything you wish.

To practice feeling these emotions, I've listed several meditations in the Resources section at the end of this book. They're all free meditations from the Insight Timer app that can help you feel positive and beneficial emotions. None of us have to walk around beating ourselves up all the time. Like anything else, with a little bit of practice, we can get really good at feeling love and much more for ourselves.

FIVE

Discovering Your Purpose

When I surveyed women about their struggles, many of them indicated they were wrestling with purpose and meaning. But figuring all that out was laced with a seemingly impossible duality: How to discover and do what they loved, and then also somehow still be a wife, mother, breadwinner, best friend, etc.

I'm focusing on women quite a bit in this chapter because so many of us seem to have a sense of our calling, or at least we understand where the disconnects are in our lives between their calling and the everyday, but we feel unable to fathom what to do with that information. Here is an excerpt from one of the surveys that sums it up perfectly:

I'm a person who charges forward once I have a goal, but getting me to see the goal and speak the goal are my obstacles. Especially when it means taking time and effort away from my family. It's that act of admitting what I already know deep down to be true that's hard for me. I feel like most of us know when there's that disconnect, even if we can't articulate it. It's just nailing it down that's so hard, because the perfect wife, mother, and woman puts other people first, or so we've been taught. So putting myself forward feels like a success and a failure at the same time.

So many women believe that if they succeed, something else will fail. And that keeps them from even beginning to even think about or acknowledge their calling.

A calling, by the way, doesn't have to be a single ginormous career or activity that you figure out once and then you're done. Most of our life experiences aren't quite so clean and simple. I've had lots of callings —novelist, editor, entrepreneur—and I'm sure there will be many more before I hang up my hat. A calling can definitely be a grand adventure or a big shift, but it might also be as simple as acknowledging that you want to take a drawing class or get more involved in your community.

When many women say, "I don't know my calling," I think 80 percent of the time it's B.S. They *do* know, they're just afraid to look at it. Because what would happen then? They imagine a future in which they're doing what they want, but somehow their family suffers, the finances go tits-up, the kids become feral, and the laundry never gets done.

In this chapter, we're going to question that story-line. Remember, the crux of writing a better life for yourself is figuring out the tension between the stories you already believe to be true, and the ones you want to be true instead. If you're writing a story where you can't fathom a life where you get to do what you want, we're going to see if there is a different narrative you can begin to pen. Remember that permission slip from earlier in the book? It applies here, too. You have permission to live the life you've imagined. And the good news is, it doesn't have to be as earth-shaking or apple-cart-upsetting as you might think.

Just Do It

In the same *SuperSoul* Conversation with Oprah and poet Mark Nepo that I referenced in Chapter Two, Mark talks about how our culture teaches us to connect *producing something* to our gifts. "If I write, someone says, 'You should be a writer.' If someone loves the land, 'You should be a gardener.' We're being turned into a noun, when the aliveness is staying a verb."

His point was that if you love something, then you can just do it. You don't have to *become* that thing. If you love to write, then just write. If you like to paint, then just paint. It doesn't have to be your career. You don't have to go back to school and get a second degree and take out a billion dollars in loans and miss seeing your kid perform in *Into the Woods* because of it. You can just do it.

I know someone who feels like they missed their calling to start a restaurant. Today, they have two kids and a partner who decidedly does not want to jump feet-first into the restaurant life, which is notoriously difficult. This person feels so stuck and so hopeless, as if their purpose is behind them and they can never go back to it.

But their story doesn't have to be so black and white. Imagine if this person simply started cooking food for others. Sure, they might have to serve it in their living room, and it might not be Michelin-rated, but who says they won't still be doing what they love? Maybe this person could cook and sell things at a local market. They might start a blog and share recipes there.

A few years ago, when I wanted to break into travel writing, I contacted an online outlet and pitched them a few story ideas. I volunteered to write one of the articles for free so they could see I had the chops for the job (and this was also a tactic to get noticed among all the other countless story submissions they were getting). I believed that once they knew I could handle the work and do it well, they would assign me other stories and pay me for them. It worked, and I wound up doing several stories for them about oddball festivals and off-the-beaten-path trails, which I loved. After that first story, they totally paid me for my work.

Now, before anyone freaks out, I'm not advocating that you swap getting paid for your livelihood by taking free gigs that are "good for visibility" or some other related nonsense. There are horror stories out there of scammers trying to take advantage of people's art and talent in exchange for publicity or non-monetary compensation. Let me be clear: When I volunteered to write that article for free, I had a full-time job that paid the bills. What I didn't have was a sense of enjoyment, adventure, or purpose in my full-time work. I felt called to do something more, and travel writing was an outlet I wanted to explore. To me, writing a story for free was a fair trade because I was trying to break into a brand-new field where I had zero experience. It would be a decidedly different story for someone with years of experience and lots of travel articles under their belt.

My point here is not that you do a ton of work for free and get taken advantage of. Rather, it's simply to ask whether there are ways you can jump in and start doing what you love without worrying about making it into something official or formal. I didn't need to become a travel writer as my official vocation. I simply wanted to do it. So I did. And you can too.

Just start. Just do the thing.

Perhaps it will *become* something official or formal, and if that's what you want, that's great! But for now, think about whether you can do what you love without concerning yourself with the outcome.

Happiness on the Side

For many years, my husband and I worked day jobs that paid the bills, all while we did side gigs that allowed us to pursue our dreams.

For more than a decade, I worked 8 to 5, Monday through Friday, at the University of Michigan, then wrote novels on the weekends. I burned through vacation time going on writers' retreats and squirreling myself away with my characters. There were years where we didn't do much socially, simply because weekends and holidays were monopolized with me at my computer, pounding out chapters.

When my first novel was published in 2009, I kept

working full-time. Same with my second novel. And my third. The full-time gig didn't end until I got a five-figure advance when I switched to from writing young-adult novels to romance novels. And even then, I found a part-time job (still at the University of Michigan) to ensure that no matter what happened, we could keep the lights on.

To this day, I *still* work that same part-time gig.

In fact, I'm working more jobs now than ever. I pay the mortgage with the Michigan job. I pay the other bills with work that comes in through my writing business. I help Rob at the ice cream store and, now, I'm starting to build *Author Your Life*.

In case it's not clear, *Author Your Life* is *not* how I'm paying the bills. It feels like the most important, most valuable thing I've ever engaged in. *It is my purpose*. But I'm not relying on it to be anything official or formal or income-generating. I'm just letting it be.

The good news is, the fact that it's so informal doesn't take any enjoyment away from it. In fact, it probably ensures I get more enjoyment from the work. I can just let the creation take shape and see what happens.

There's no shame in having a job that pays the bills and gives you a sense of security, and then doing what you love as a side gig. Again, if you want it to become your primary vocation and the way that you generate the majority of your income, that's awesome! That is totally possible. You can write a story where that happens, too. But there's no shame in starting small.

My friend Jess started a business called Cool Critters

where she sews funny, funky little stuffed animal monsters that are cute and strange and wonderful. She did this gig on the side for years, going to craft shows on weekends and sewing in her spare time. Today, it's a full-time, money-making business and she's hiring her first employee. Exciting stuff! But it all started small. It all started because she loved making strange little stuffed animals that she'd never seen anyone do before. It was her calling, and she simply answered it without worrying where it would eventually lead.

The Gift of Time

Maybe Jess's story isn't quite resonating with you because you're wondering how you could fold one more thing into your already busy life—even something as important as fulfilling your purpose. And I totally get that. Our society isn't exactly wired to help women think about how they can focus on themselves and their needs. In fact, it's pretty much the opposite.

We are saddled with the expectation that we'll be accomplished but not so accomplished that we become prideful and forget our place; be outspoken but not raise our voices so much that we're a bossy bitch; be fun and easygoing but still check off all the items on our to-do list. Oh, and of course look beautiful while we do it all. Women bear the majority of the literal and emotional labor of supporting and caretaking for families, kids, and colleagues—and yet we wonder why we get to the end of the day with no gas left in the tank.

The reality is that if you don't prioritize yourself and

find a way to give yourself the gift of time, there's a good chance your purpose is going to slip through your grasp. I understand if you don't have much bandwidth. But can you carve out pockets of time for yourself to simply start doing the thing you love? Here are some ideas:

- Turn off the TV
- Take social media off your phone and set time limits for how much you use it
- Practice saying no to anything that doesn't fill you with delight
- Enroll your kids in fewer activities
- Hire a housekeeper
- Hire a babysitter
- If money is tight, perhaps do a trade that can free up some time and space
- Revisit your permission slip every day

Someone is Waiting for You

Women are great at serving others and putting themselves last. If that's your default mode, you're not alone.

But putting yourself last all the time will ultimately be more hurtful than helpful. Not just to you and your heart, but to the people who need you. And I don't just mean your family or close friends. I'm talking about the person out there who is waiting for you to take hold of your purpose and absolutely own it because they *need* the gifts and talents you bring to the world. They need to see your art. To read your stories. To get your help organizing their finances or to start their company. They need you and what you offer. You're their Avenger. Their Wonder Woman. Their Buffy. And when you hold back and refuse to answer the call, you're leaving someone in the lurch who is counting on you.

How Will I Know? What if I'm Wrong?

Many women whom I surveyed had plenty of anxiety about whether and how they would know if they were on the right track with their purpose. How would they know if the timing was right? What if they got it wrong? One woman wrote:

I'm wondering if I should continue with [my current path], or if I should go off in another direction. I do feel like the lessons life that has given me can be used to do good in the world, but I just don't know which way to go.

That moment when you're standing at the forked path in the woods wondering which way to go can be terrifying. But there's no right or wrong, no black or white. Either path is okay. *Every* path is okay. It all can be used for your highest good.

When I started *Lara's Life* in early 2018, I was in the process of building a new company, and many of my book's chapters were about that company's success.

I'd started a business with the killer idea to help nonprofits raise money and not spend a ton in the process. Nonprofits often have to stretch their already thin budgets to hire someone like me to write a brochure or annual appeal or website that makes folks want to give. So I thought, instead, why not package my expertise, then sell it in a toolkit for a single, low price. And then the nonprofit could re-use that toolkit any time they needed it at no extra cost. Great idea, right? So I did it and launched it and, at the end of the day, it was a total flop.

No matter how much I tried rolling that business boulder up the hill, I was Sisyphus, never making it to the top. No matter how many pages I wore out in *Lara's Life* trying to manifest abundance with my company, it didn't come to pass. I was striving so hard, I was working my tail off, and it was exhausting. The model I had envisioned just didn't work. A toolkit, while great in theory, just isn't the way busy nonprofits want or need to be helped. Worse, every time I tried something like a class or a webinar, it didn't just *not* go well. It was like I was cursed.

Time and time again, I felt not just unsupported by the universe, but actively thwarted. What the heck was going on? This was heartbreaking and infuriating. I thought I had screwed up. I had missed my calling.

Except not quite.

As a result of this series of failures, I went back to the drawing board. What was I actually here to do? What brought me joy? One of the things that came up was how much I loved working on *Author Your Life*. When I thought about what made me happy, it always came back to this book, and the power of words and stories. This was a big sign that *Author Your Life* was possibly more than just an experiment I was undertaking—it was going to be a way to help others, too. I don't think I would have ever realized how important *Author Your Life* was if my business model had succeeded.

What's more, while this particular business model as I'd envisioned it was doomed, the process of launching it taught me a new skillset, including how to create and publish webinars, how to create online sales pages, and how to package and sell toolkits. In particular, I loved creating these toolkits, and bringing them into the world had brought me tons of satisfaction. You can bet that I'm pulling on that skillset now as I write this book and put it into the world. I'm a thousand percent certain that part of what the universe wanted for me in that process was to stretch myself and my skills so I could use them with *Author Your Life*.

And, throughout this whole journey, the universe still brought me paying clients and ensured I was taken care of. It's not like I wasn't making any money from my business—I just wasn't making it in the way I had planned. There was still so much to be thankful for.

It took me almost a year to figure all this out, but it doesn't have to take you that long. There were signs along the way that I missed because my eyes weren't open, but I'm giving you the roadmap so you can see them. Here are a few ways to know if you're on the right track with your purpose:

- **Things feel easy**. There's joy and delight in the work, and it's not a slog every minute of every day. If things are consistently tough or always seem to be going wrong, hit the pause button now because the universe is trying to get your attention.

- **Time flies**. Five hours feels like five minutes. Work doesn't feel like work. Instead, it seems like you were in a different and wonderful world.

- **It's abundant.** In joy, in meaning, in wonder. It can ultimately be abundant financially if that's what you want it to be, though again I'd caution anyone to start out small. No matter the scale of what you're doing, you're absolutely receiving fulfillment.

- **"Coincidences" occur.** The universe loves to cheerlead us when we start living a connected and meaningful life. "I can't believe that just happened!" will be a regular part of your vocabulary when you're on the right track.

How to Find Your Purpose and Infuse Your Life with More Meaning

Exercise #1: The Heart Knows

Are you unsure of your purpose, or would you like more clarity? If so, grab your notebook and a pen, and sit down. Take a deep breath. There's part of you that's been trying to get your attention for a while now, but hasn't been able to be heard. Now, you feel it, and you are ready to listen. It calls your name. Write the following sentence:

[Your Name], this is your heart. I hold your truest desires, and I see the future you want most. It looks like this…

Just see what comes next. Your heart will tell you what it needs. Your heart will fill in the blanks. Your heart knows your highest calling, your truest purpose, and what fulfillment looks like.

The power in this exercise isn't that our highest self will speak to us if we let it. That's a given. The power in this exercise is that we make time to listen.

Exercise #2: Write Your Story Around Your Heart's Calling

One of the dreams I have about *Author Your Life* is that it will be able to reach and help people all over the world. I have called the entire concept of *Author Your Life* my Oprah-Sized Idea because it's just that big.

In my own story, one of the chapters I've written is about how I do a *SuperSoul* Conversation with Oprah. She does all her podcasting in Hawaii, so many times on the recordings you can hear birds chirping and tropical leaves rustling. I have imagined myself sitting in that beautiful space with her, feeling the warm breeze, my heart full to bursting because we're having such an incredible conversation about the power of words and stories. Here are some of the details I wrote in Lara's Life about the *SuperSoul* Conversation:

Lara and Oprah are in a beautiful and sacred-feeling grove of trees. There is a bright blue sky above them and the hush of ocean waves in the distance. Birds chirp and flowers bloom in bold colors all around them. Lara tells Oprah how the Hero's Journey isn't just a convenient storytelling template—it's a law of the universe. Oprah is delighted by this.

This is such an audacious and bold dream! But it's so vivid and real. I can see this story so clearly. It's in my heart, in my mind, and now it's on paper. This is the way it begins to happen in real life.

Now, it's your turn.

Let's say, for example, that you're feeling unfulfilled in your job and your heart is calling you to find a new one. Try writing a story where you find your dream job with ease, and where you love your new gig and have meaningful work to do.

To start, write down as much detail as you want about your new job, about how much money you make, or what you wear when you land this fabulous new gig. What does your office look like? Do you wave to your new colleagues when you step off the elevator?

Whatever it is, picture it in your mind's eye and really describe it. The smells, the colors, what is happening while you're there, and what you feel. Are you sitting at the kitchen table knitting? Are you in a pottery class with your hands covered in clay? Perhaps you're at a computer designing websites for small businesses.

Whatever your heart told you in the previous exercise, it's now time to create a story around it.

. . .

Exercise #3: Create Opportunities

It's never too late to bust down doors of opportunity and do more of what you love. The challenge, of course, is that it often feels so overwhelming to engage something new. Where to even start?

You may be looking to learn about a new field or meet like-minded people. Perhaps you want to try something for the first time, or maybe you need to figure out how something even works. In other words, you need information and connections and *help*.

Therefore, in your book, you will want to write that whatever you need begins to show itself. For example: *[Your Name] begins meeting the right people who can help her [do a specific activity or learn a specific thing]. She is amazed by how they show up when she needs them. Her eyes are open to seeing them, and she is not afraid to connect with them.*

Maybe you don't need a person but you need a class. Or a community. That's okay too. You can write that whatever you need comes into your life, and that your eyes are open to see it so you don't miss it.

Some very practical ways to connect to opportunities and your purpose might also be right in front of you. Don't overlook:

Volunteering. It's a great way to learn about a new topic and meet new people. And volunteering isn't just about helping nonprofits. Let's say you want to stick a toe into computers and coding. Try volunteering for a tech event (like a code marathon) where you can help out while also connecting with people who are in the industry. If it's not a love match, no worries! You're not out anything except a few hours of time. And if it is, then great! You met some folks and helped out and started learning about the field.

Informational Interviewing. People love to talk about themselves and what they do. Do you want to find out about how to break into a certain job or what a new career might be like? Tell someone actually doing it that you think their job is fascinating and you want to learn all you can. Informational interviewing isn't about getting a job or ultimately gaining something. It's about listening and taking in someone else's story so you can apply it to your own journey. Right now, there may be a voice inside your head saying, "Oh, that person would never want to talk to me," but I bet you'll be surprised. People are excited when others take an interest in them, so reach out and see what happens.

Networking. This word doesn't mean going to events and pressing your business card into people's hands in a sales-y, disingenuous way. Rather, this is about meeting and connecting to people not for what they can do for you, but because you have something in common or because you share a genuine connection. Even if your calling is to do something as solitary as writing, you still need other people—to read and critique your work, to learn about the industry, to discuss the changing face of publishing, and more. You can't achieve your purpose 100 percent on your own, cut off from humanity.

. . .

Exercise #4: Investigate the Story Behind "I Have No Time"

Oh, you didn't think I was going to stop talking about the whole "give yourself more time" thing, did you?

If you don't have the time or can't imagine having the time to engage the purpose deep in your heart, it's okay. The truth is that you probably do have the time, but something else is holding you back. Maybe fear. Maybe uncertainty.

For the longest while, I would complain about how much freelance work I had, and my heart was often a cesspool of resentment about it. It kept me so busy! It was never finished!

I felt on the edge of insanity every minute. I would cross one project off my to-do list, only to be faced with another. I would think, "I can't do this," only to wake up and do it all over again the next day.

Of course, as the owner of my own business, I was in charge of how much work I took on—but I felt like I could never say no to anything. So often, we needed the money just to keep the lights on. I was on a treadmill, never getting anywhere.

Then one day, as I was meditating, and I saw a big, fat tree root in my mind's eye. This root was branded, and the writing burned into said: *Fear of more work.*

I knew instantly this was my root.

It was central to what was "holding me up," so to speak.

It had grown into the center of my being through old stories filled with fear and bad feelings. Those stories said that when you work hard, you're automatically a victim: you're unappreciated, taken for granted, unseen, and generally bulldozed. I learned this story from my family growing up, and when I saw that root in my mind's eye, I understood that this story had never left me. In that moment, I realized it wasn't the freelance projects that were keeping me on the endless treadmill of work—it was me and my belief in an old story.

This old story made me feel like every project was an all-consuming slog, every client was someone who just didn't get it. I was so scared of work because it meant I would feel taken advantage of and stepped on all over again. Even when the work wasn't difficult, even when the client was a delight, there was part of me that made it miserable because I was filtering it through the lens of outdated beliefs. Even if a project didn't take up much time, I let it *feel* consuming, because I was letting the old story drive the narrative.

When I saw this story for what it was, I immediately put pen to paper to write a new one. I wrote about how happy I was to get up in the morning and start my job. I wrote about how full my heart felt with gratitude, because I was getting gigs that paid the bills. I wrote about how I could listen to clients openly and to see them with love and thankfulness instead of resentment. I wrote about how I had more time because projects were a breeze to complete.

In my mind, I pictured the root and told it how thankful I was for all its effort holding me up for all these years. But I told it its work was done. Different roots were going to come in now and relieve it of its duty. Those roots were joy, compassion, understanding, listening, gratitude, and more.

Today, my work feels so much more balanced. I'm not scrambling all the time to do *all the things*. My level of work hasn't changed—but my mind has. I have so much more peace and enjoyment with every project, not to mention ease.

Most importantly, I'm not always racing against the clock, resentful that I can't ever get ahead. A direct outcome of re-writing this old story is feeling like I have *much more* time.

If you feel like you're on a treadmill that you can't get off, something internal is driving you. I promise you, it's not kids' activities or volunteer commitments or the number of holiday parties you've been invited to. At root (pun intended) is an old story that you've told yourself for so long that you absolutely believe it.

If you're ready to uncover and change that story, simply start by writing one sentence: *[Your Name] has the time to pursue her purpose.*

It sounds so simple, but just writing that down has the power to begin to change things. And if you want to, you can do this for anything you want to do in life, you don't have to limit it to your purpose:

[Your Name] has time to take piano lessons.

[Your Name] has time to read for pleasure.

Then, try to spot the moments when you're feeling crazy, harried, overwhelmed, angry, fearful, at your wits' end, or so resentful you could punch something. You might not be able to do it in that moment, but maybe later, when you've calmed down and had a sandwich, try to poke around and investigate what stories you were telling yourself at that time. Is it that you have to do everything or it won't get done? Is it that you don't deserve to have an hour to yourself? Is it that working hard means you're a sucker and you're getting taken advantage of?

If you can understand the stories you're already telling yourself, then you can begin to write new ones that change the narrative.

The goal is to challenge these old beliefs. Because chances are, they're not true. And you can write a better story that can go in their place.

Exercise #5: Question "I Never," "I Can't," or "I Always"

Many of us think in black and white terms (God knows I do!), and it can be a dangerous thing. If you *always* or *never* or *can't* do something, you've already made up your mind about who you are and how you operate. There's no room for change.

In one survey response, I heard from a woman who was unhappy in her work, and definitively told me this about her career path: *There's no possible way I will find a job that uses my education and experience, where I can make sure I will be able to provide for my family.*

The truth is, there might be something out there for her. In fact, I believe that there could be a way for her to feel less trapped and to engage in more meaningful work. There might even be something she could do on the side that would infuse her with so much happiness that it would make her day job more tolerable. But if she's already decided that none of it is possible, then there's no chance of it happening.

It doesn't have to be like this. The first step is recognizing this kind of stinkin' thinkin' when it happens so that you can change it.

To identify black-and-white thinking, reflect for a moment on areas of your life that feel impossible, immovable, rigid, or unyielding.

What are those areas? Are there parts of your personality that you define yourself by (for instance, I'm always sarcastic! I always say yes!), but that could just be defense mechanisms or the result of fear?

I recently uncovered a deeply held belief that I can't be too visible or bold, because I owe penance for my mistakes. It's like a ticker-tape of thinking along the lines of, "I've screwed up and I need to constantly atone for it."

Whether I was a jerk to someone in grade school or I said the wrong thing in a meeting once or I accidentally tripped on the sidewalk two years ago—you name it, I had to atone for it. The way I did that was to hold myself back from being an expert or owning the room, because people would figure out I'd screwed up and would be like, "She can't be an awesome writer, she did that *one thing* that *one time*." As a result, I'd diminish my capabilities and my expertise, believing this would help me not be "found out."

I discovered this pattern because I've been writing a story where I'm front and center, teaching about *Author*

Your Life and totally owning this space. There is really no way to write about reaching and helping lots of people with this book and to not see the patterns in my old stories and thinking emerge.

I'm changing my story of "I can't..." into "Oh hell yes I will."

Now, your turn!

Write out a story that goes like this: *[Your Name] recognizes when she is thinking in black and white terms. She sees the patterns clearly and she doesn't run from them. She considers whether the things she's telling herself are actually true. She is filled with more hope and possibility. Opportunities come to her. She believes the best, and feels joy, hope, and optimism.*

Changing your thinking about anything takes time and, like everything else, the more you practice it, the more effective it will be. Your heart is calling to you to do more of what you love, and there's happiness, freedom, and fulfillment on the other side of saying yes.

In note

Use this "story line" when we get stuck from fear or old stories ⚹

73

SIX

Achieving Financial Abundance

There is no other area of *Lara's Life* that kicked my butt like money did. I had so much work to do in this area—and I'll be honest, I'm still clearing my way through a lot of debris. I had 43 years of bad money lessons to unlearn, so naturally it's taking me more than 12 months to really get a handle on all of this. To this day, I keep working on my money story.

Money is such a clear divining rod for how the universe works and how, when we say what we want, the universe wants to make sure that we're serious. Money was one of the first areas that really showed me that *Author Your Life* worked. There was such a clear, direct correlation between telling the universe that I wanted financial abundance and Hero's Journey trials that immediately followed. I knew the connection couldn't be a coincidence.

Here's what went down.

Early in *Lara's Life*, I wrote about how Lara paid every bill with ease, how she felt so excited when she looked at her bank account, and how she was filled with gratitude every time she saw her balance. I wrote about how Lara had the ability to buy what she needed and wanted, which included a new couch, since ours was literally falling apart. *Lara's Life* included money for travel and the ability to be a financial blessing to others.

I am the main breadwinner for our home and, at the time, even though I had a steady paycheck through my part-time Michigan job, it wasn't all that much money. The health insurance was the real benefit, so my free-lance income was what kept us afloat. And right away, there was unexpected red tape with my biggest client. I'd been paid regularly by this client for months, but suddenly that steady check that kept the mortgage paid was nowhere to be found.

At the exact same time, our beloved Labrador, Oliver, got very sick. It may be worth noting here that Rob and I don't have kids, and Oliver was a central figure in our family. I came home one day to find his back legs had simply stopped working.

We rushed him to the vet the next morning, and they recommended he go see a specialist for a more thorough diagnosis. Let me tell you how *not* cheap that was. They kept him overnight for supervision, then kept on holding him, because he couldn't go to the bathroom on his own and he needed a ton of hands-on care. Days went by, while we agonized about what to do and whether or not we could save him. In the meantime, we just kept racking up vet charges.

By the time we realized Oliver was beyond help and we had to have him put down, the whole thing had cost us multiple thousands of dollars. Oh, and did I mention the part where I suddenly wasn't getting paid?

As if this shit sandwich weren't big enough already, we went to get our taxes done at this time and discovered we owed $10,000. I remember the dazed feeling I had when we left the accountant's office. They had put us on a payment plan for the money we owed for federal taxes, but we still had to fork over a big chunk of money out-of-pocket to pay off the state.

We'd scooped out our savings just to pay regular bills and get by, and we'd had to tap into our deep savings (you know, that account that's harder to access, that you only pull on in emergencies?) just to pay for Oliver. We were so completely out of money it wasn't even funny. We couldn't even put this on credit cards because we'd maxed out our credit opening Rob's ice cream business, and we had almost zero room on any card for anything.

Smack dab in the middle of this, Rob had to have surgery. Now, I just finished telling you that I had a part-time job specifically for health insurance, so this should be no big deal, right? Except out of the blue, the insurance company was saying that it was going to cost us $3,000 out of pocket, in addition to what they would cover.

At this moment, you couldn't have *written* a more perfect plot point. In fact, if I had submitted a novel to my agent about a woman who decides she is ready to receive financial abundance in her life and then goes on to experience financial calamity, my agent probably would have sent it back with the note, "Too on the nose. Needs nuance."

This financial tornado of suck wasn't a coincidence. This was part of the process. It's true that I wanted financial abundance. I wanted the new couch and the travel fund and ease paying my bills. And there's nothing wrong with wanting that stuff. But I had to learn a few things first before I could receive them, and that's what the universe was trying to teach me.

The lessons included believing I was worthy of making money. In the chapter on loving yourself, I talked about how, by May, our financial fortunes had reversed. Indeed, I was making more money than I ever had. But I couldn't hold onto it. I repelled it and spent it because, deep down, my inner garbage person didn't think I deserved it.

I also had a big, fat chip on my shoulder that *expected* the universe to bless me, as if I was owed something. This idea of abundance being my due made my heart extremely hard, and it prevented me from being grateful for what I *did* have. When we think we're owed, we're always hungry for the next thing, and never satisfied with the metaphorical meal we've just been served. This was me—a bottomless pit of "nothing is enough" because I was trying to cover my inner garbage person with riches, while continually scanning the horizon for my next paycheck.

Money was a giant mirror that reflected back to me all the ways I needed to change. For me, achieving financial abundance was never about spreadsheets and budgeting, although that stuff is important, too. At its foundation, my financial journey required that I nurture a heart and personality and mindset that could both attract and keep money. I had to change my insides before anything would change on the outside.

The good news is that, today, my financial path gets lighter and brighter every minute. For example, at the start of *Lara's Life*, I'd written out two incredibly ambitious financial goals that would clear out almost $40,000 worth of debt from our books. That just came to pass at the tail end of 2018. (Way to slide it in under the wire, universe! Thank you!) Rob and I are healthier and happier than we've ever been. We've learned to tackle financial calamities together, to communicate, and to realize that we are stronger as a team than we are apart.

Best of all, I feel different. More grateful and much more at peace. I have more trust that the universe has my back.

We don't quite have the new couch yet, but I keep writing a story where we get it.

How to Write Your Story of Financial Abundance

Exercise #1: Maintaining an Attitude of Gratitude

As a general rule, if you want more of anything, the best way to get it is to be supremely thankful for everything you have *now*. As I learned the hard way, the universe doesn't really like to bless people who expect it and then aren't grateful when their fortune shows up.

Having more gratitude has made me happier, more

present, more tender, and more able to see the good things all around me. Finances aside, I would encourage anyone to make gratitude part of their story every day. There is just no downside to more of it.

If you're reading this and you're in the middle of an epic crapstorm that makes it feel like life is slinging poo at your face every five seconds, it can seem nigh on impossible to get *thankful* for all you're going through. In fact, the very idea might make you want to throat-punch this book. At the darkest part of my financial crisis, when I was exhausted and beat-up and feeling like a failure in just about every sense, I was the same way. I was raging on the inside: Why me? What did I ever do to deserve this?

Turns out that my anger and fury and feelings of injustice never changed anything. It was only when I surrendered and said, "Okay, universe. You win. I have something to learn here and I will learn it," that the Titanic of a ship that was our financial course could finally, ever so slowly, begin to turn.

Surrender is a word I'm going to talk more about in the Change section of this book, and I think surrender and gratitude are very close cousins. For now, try rooting around and grabbing onto something in your life that doesn't blow. Something that is still good, even in the midst of the awfulness. There is always something for which we can say thank you.

Now, to kick off your new gratitude story, write that simple line in your book that has the power to change everything:

[You Name] is grateful for all she has in her life.

Just like in the section about loving yourself, where I encouraged you to write that you love yourself every day, I want you to do the same thing with gratitude. Make it part of your story every time you sit down to write. It's also easy to add to. Think about all the things that you have in your life that are going right. For example, you're breathing and reading this book! That means a.) you're alive! and b.) you can read! Or you can at least *listen* if you struggle with reading and are getting all this through an audiobook. That means you can add to your story:

[Your Name] is thankful for all the blessings that surround her. Her eyes are open to the ways in which she is blessed and already abundant. [Now, list some of the blessings in your life and things you have to be grateful for.]

As an example, here is one chapter on gratitude from *Lara's Life*, which I wrote in the throes of financial despair:

No matter what, Lara gives thanks for all she has. Her heart remains grateful. Lara gives thanks for her home, for her community, for her husband, for her little dog, for opportunities, for technology, for physical wellness, for a great local library, for caring parents, for food to eat and access to local farms, for cars that run and are safe, for friendships, for opportunities to write and make money, for good books, and for abundance in spades.

I was feeling despair and hopelessness when I wrote that, but when I saw those words, it helped me realize how much I truly had, and it helped my mindset begin to shift.

. . .

Exercise #2: Feel that Gratitude, Baby!

Gratitude is one of the areas where we need to connect to our insides and feel it baby, yeah. It's one thing to list what you're thankful for, as we did above; it's another thing to let your heart really experience all of that awesomeness.

After you write out some of the things that you're thankful for, I want you to close your eyes and put your hand on your heart. Take some deep breaths, and see in your mind's eye all the things you just wrote. Feel that gratitude and tell the universe "thank you" for all that you have. Let your heart soften and fill up. Speak the words "thank you" at least three times out loud.

If this is tough for you, I get it. Feelings are hard! To help jump-start this area, I've listed some gratitude meditations in the resource section of this book. Letting an experienced teacher guide me toward feelings of gratitude has been a game-changer.

Exercise #3 Trust that You Are Taken Care Of

At one point in my journey, I was working a freelance gig that was really lucrative, but it had become a soul-sucking slog. The person I reported to was a micromanager, and they'd endlessly critique—or outright reject—all my work. Now, I'm all for constructive criticism, but this was a creativity-stifling environment where very few new ideas were being embraced or encouraged.

This gig was hollowing out my insides. But the problem was, it paid well. I didn't know how we'd get by without it. I couldn't see a way to continue with it, and I couldn't see a way to walk away from it.

Yet I could feel the energy shifting around this high-paying gig. I could feel my heart saying, "It's time to go." I had nothing lined up to replace it. Nothing but the certainty in my soul that it was right to leave.

When I looked at *Lara's Life* and the stories there, I saw someone who loved her work and was energized by it. I saw someone surrounded by like-minded people who encouraged and nurtured her. I didn't see someone slaving away at a lifeless gig just to keep the mortgage paid.

It was terrifying, but I released that job. I put in my two weeks and said I was moving on. The minute I did, more work came my way. This work was more enjoyable, more engaging, and it made me a thousand times happier.

I know many people reading this feel like they don't have the luxury of leaving their misery-making jobs right now—not with families to support and insurance to keep. Please know: I'm not telling you to do that, but rather I'm saying that **when we listen to our hearts and act in accordance with what's there, the universe rushes in to help us**. For me, when I left that crappy job, the universe sent me more freelance gigs. For you, if you're stuck in a sucky job, it might be that the universe leads you to new opportunities and connections that help you begin to believe that there's something better out there.

I'm not saying flip the double bird to your boss and walk out today if you're depending on that income.

Instead, begin to write a new story that leads you to something better in, say, six months. Trust that the universe wants to bless you: With more money. More happiness. More fulfillment. Because it totally does. The universe is on your side.

So get out your pens and start that new, awesome story.

[Your Name] is taken care of by the universe. She knows deep down that the universe is working on her behalf, not against her. She has wisdom about when to make her moves, and she has faith that she is taken care of at every step.

Do you need a job that brings you more money? Write a story where you get it, and you have the courage go for that new gig when you need to leap.

Do you need help clearing out debt from your life? Write a story where you are debt free and you take hold of debt-clearing opportunities when they're presented to you.

When you step Indiana Jones-style onto the bridge that your heart tells you is there, the universe will catch you. Every time.

Exercise #4: Accessing the Resources You Need

When I started writing my financial story, I was amazed at the resources that started coming into my life, because they were exactly what I needed.

For the longest time, I'd had an email from a friend sitting in my inbox. It contained a link to the website of Denise Duffield-Thomas, an incredible money guru. This email had gone unopened for months, but then suddenly I just *knew* I was supposed to click it. I did, and Denise has become one of my go-to teachers for clearing what she calls "money blocks." I list both of her books in the Resources section of this book, and I can't recommend her enough (and I'll talk about her more in the "Meeting the Mentors" section of the book).

Denise was just one example of the countless resources, people, books, podcasts, and shows that came into my life when I needed them. Not just about money, but about everything. This is such an incredible phenomenon, because it's more proof that the universe has our back on our journey. When we start writing a better story for ourselves, the universe will send us the help we need to get there. We just have to be open to receiving it.

In the previous chapter on purpose, I talked about networking and how it can lead to people who can help us figure out what we want to do in life. Well, it can also lead to financial opportunities, as it did for me. When I was looking to expand my business and make more money, I started talking to friends about it, and those friends connected me to other friends. I got off my butt and had coffee and met folks and just *got out there* into the world and explained more about what I did. And this opened so many doors! I didn't expect anything when I met these new people—but many of those connections ultimately led to money-making gigs.

If that feels overwhelming and you're just not sure where to start, I got you. Because you start here, by writing this in your book:

[Your Name] has the resources she needs at every stage of

her journey. Her eyes are open to seeing and accessing the help she needs. She has the courage to learn and change to get where she wants to go.

Do you know what specific resource you need to break through to a new financial level? Maybe it's a class or a book or a mastermind group. If so, get specific and write a story where you get the thing you need.

And if you don't know precisely what you need (like I sure didn't), then it's fine to keep it more general.

The great news is, you don't have to worry about *how* these resources get to you. You just have to write your story and do the work of keeping your eyes open —for online groups, for real-life meet-ups, for books, for podcasts, and for getting off your butt and getting out into the world when you have the opportunity.

Exercise #5: Paint that Picture

Do you know what it looks like when you have financial abundance? How about what it feels like?

In *Lara's Life*, I wrote about how great it felt to have enough to pay our bills. I wrote about how my work was both enjoyable and lucrative. I also wasn't afraid to dream even bigger. For example, one of the audacious, long-term dreams that Rob and I have is to someday own a home in northern Michigan. When I started *Lara's Life*, I started writing in specific detail about this home. Here is an excerpt from one of my chapters:

Lara holds a steaming mug of coffee and looks out a wall of beautiful windows to a picturesque backyard with trees and water. It's Northern Michigan and all around her is peace and the thick blanket of silence that comes from being in nature. Light streams in. The room she's in is filled with white and blue tones. Lara moves to the nearby table and begins her day wearing beautiful clothes that are also comfortable. She feels ease and gratitude to be doing this work. It is financially abundant and she checks her bank account just so she can give thanks to the universe for all she has...

In the story of your life, you can paint a picture of what financial abundance looks like to you. You can write about everything from being able to pay your bills with ease and joy to being able to help others because you're so blessed to being able to take hold of your long-term dreams.

Trust me, the universe listens. Within a matter of weeks of doing this work, I had a friend who gave me her key to her cottage in northern Michigan. They were moving, and they knew they weren't going to be using it as much. I nearly toppled over. It's such a gift and a blessing! Someday we'd still love to have our own place, but in the meantime, this was such a tangible confirmation that the universe is listening.

So close your eyes. See that picture in your head. Feel what it's like. And then write down that story.

SEVEN

Connecting to Your Body and Health

Our bodies are such powerful, amazing vessels and yet we're taught to loathe them from the time we're little. This is especially true for women and, again, ladies are a big focus of this chapter. That's because we're told very early on that our bodies are either not enough— not skinny enough, not tall enough, not hot enough—or that they're too much—too sexy, too fat, too hairy, you name it.

For those of us who have tried to make our bodies conform to the narrow middle ground between these dualities, it has inevitably resulted in misery. That's because finding such a narrow middle ground is nearly impossible. Be hot but not slutty. Be fit but not bulky. Be yourself but not too individual. GAH! Cue bad story after bad story that needs a re-write!

When I started *Lara's Life*, I initially wrote a lot of chapters in my story about losing weight, because it was the most obvious and glaring thing I wanted to "fix." For example, *Lara loses X pounds by X date*. Or *Lara goes to Weight Watchers and this time it works*.

But pretty quickly into the process, weight was shoved onto the backburner. In its place, what came into sharp focus was a new story that had me connecting more with my body, listening to myself, forgiving myself, and loving myself. Did I lose weight in the process of writing *Lara's Life*? Yep, you bet. But let me be clear: It was a byproduct. It didn't come because I went to Weight Watchers and finally figured out how to work the program. It happened because I learned that the weight wasn't the problem, nor should it be a focus of my story.

So let me say this as we really get going into this chapter:

SCREW YOUR WEIGHT.

The last thing I'm going to do is tell you how to use *Author Your Life* to shed pounds. There are so many reasons for this, not the least of which is that there are curvy women who might be reading this who are healthy, and skinny women who are on the verge of a heart attack. If I stepped on a scale tomorrow at the doctor's office, I'd be considered obese by medical standards (measuring Body Mass Index or BMI). But let me tell you: I could drop everything right now and run a 10k without blinking, I eat great food, and I am incredibly healthy.

Author Your Life isn't a diet, and diets don't work anyway. That's because if you don't accept and love yourself now, then losing weight won't change that. There won't be a number on the scale where you feel good. So instead, this chapter is going to focus on body acceptance, and about making peace with ourselves so that we can get the nourishment we need—inside and out.

What is Health?

So, okay, let's start here with a basic definition of health. It's not a number on the scale, and it's not a plan where you eat vegetables and take vitamins. Health is a lot more complicated than that. To be healthy in your body, I believe you need to also be healthy in your mind. Connecting those two things is the focus of this chapter.

Ultimately, the goal here is to use the *Author Your Life* process to recognize when you're being a dick to your body and then to write a better story where you a.) figure out why you're being a dick to your body and b.) stop being a dick to your body. In this process, we'll continue the radical work of connecting with and loving ourselves. Because it really does all flow from there.

Obviously I'm not a doctor and this is not a medical book. If you are struggling with physical ailments, mental health issues, or disorders of any kind, please seek help from a professional. The information and exercises in this chapter can complement but should not replace care from a trained healthcare provider.

Connection Not Conquering

Deep down, when I started writing a better story for myself, the thing I wanted most was to feel good in my body. To feel like I was enough and *it* was enough. To achieve that, I began to listen to what my body was actually telling me. Instead of dragging my body to Weight Watchers every week and trying to mold my body into a different shape, I paused and got quiet. I tried to spend time hearing what was happening inside of me.

As it turns out, the messages my body was sending me were very different than what *I* was telling it. The messages it was sending me weren't things I had been hearing. I was so busy trying to yell at it to be what I needed it to be, that I hadn't been tuning in.

Like everything else, I started with the basics (because I didn't know what else to do). It was insanely simple. In *Lara's Life*, I just started writing words such as: *Lara loves and respects her body. Lara appreciates her body and when she looks at it, she sees beauty. She is not critical but instead is grateful.*

If you haven't yet read the chapter on loving yourself, please go back and read it and do the exercises in that chapter. They are truly the building blocks for everything that we're talking about here.

After I wrote the basics, I did a profound exercise. I started a letter to myself *from* my body, and just let the pen start writing, trusting that the words would come from the parts of my body that needed to speak. And did they ever. I began the letter as follows:

Dear Lara,

This is your body. And this is what I want to tell you.

Then, I just took a breath and kept writing. What came out of me was so surprising.

Please respect me. Love me. I am crying out for this. Please treat me like you would treat someone you really cherished and cared about. You would give them all the best things, and you wouldn't force them to take things they didn't want.

Now, I had to really think about that for a minute. What did that mean? In my mind, I ate healthily. I worked out. What was my body saying? What was the message?

It was at this moment that it really started to hit me how much I was drinking. That line about forcing my body to *take things it didn't want*—I believed that line was about alcohol.

When I looked closer, I'd been kidding myself about how much booze I was consuming. I'd have three glasses of wine at night pretty regularly, and plenty of alcohol on the weekends. I was buzzed a lot. More than I realized. But it wasn't until my body was begging me to stop putting poison in it that I was like, "Oh, this might be too much."

Sometimes, the *Author Your Life* process boils down to taking the time and space to be honest with ourselves. Sometimes it's just about getting real about how we're behaving and what we're actually doing (versus what we tell ourselves we're doing). This was one such case for me. I woke up to the fact that I was simply drinking too much.

Now, it's one thing to realize we're engaging in unhealthy behaviors. And it's quite another thing to stop those behaviors. That's because the behavior isn't the problem. The behavior is a sign pointing to an underlying issue that is trying to get our attention. There is some part of us that needs to be noticed, or needs love, or needs healing. So while we can force ourselves to change our behaviors for a time, unless we deal with the underlying root of what is causing us to do what we're doing, chances are we're going to go right back to the same old patterns.

In my case, alcohol was a great way to numb a whole host of feelings that I didn't know how to deal with. There was *fear* that I wasn't enough or doing things right in my life. There was *worry* and *anxiety* about our finances and whether we were going to be okay with our businesses. There was *pain* from past wounds that I still had to look at and heal. Alcohol— and to a lesser extent food—was how I comforted myself when these awful and overwhelming feelings arose.

Alcohol and food might not be your go-to comforts. You might struggle with other things, and wherever you're at is a-okay. The point is not that we share the exact same difficulties, but rather that we simply recognize them and begin to address them.

When I tackled this in *Lara's Life*, I wanted to tell myself not to feel the emotions I was having. Instead of being sad, I wanted to just write *Lara is happy!!!!!* And boom—I wanted to be happy.

But that wasn't the way forward. I realized I needed to give my feelings space and time, to listen to them and allow them to rise to the surface. I was drinking to mask all kinds of pain. Now, it was time to bring that pain to the surface. I wasn't asking the pain to go away. I was asking the pain if I could look at it and ultimately love it.

In the process of doing this, I went five months without drinking so that I could be more present with my feelings. At the end of 2018, I allowed myself a small glass of champagne on New Year's Eve. It's late January as I write this, and I will be dry again until May, when I have plans to have a beer on a trip up north. For me, cutting out alcohol this severely was the right move and one that has really helped, because moderation isn't exactly my strong suit. I've been more present, more able to feel, even if sometimes those feelings are wildly uncomfortable.

It all started with creating the story I wanted to be true on the page. That's when I began to heal and change. When I wrote, for example, about how much I loved my body or loved myself, I began to see to the disparity between the words on the page and the stark reality of how much I actually hated myself, and how I was poisoning my body. When I could finally see the reality, then I could start to change it.

The Self-Sabotage Surprise

In general, we think that people who struggle with bad behaviors engage in those bad behaviors when things go *wrong* in their lives. But as I grew more and more in tune with what I was feeling and when, I began to notice that I had the most trouble when things went right in my life.

For example, if I wrote about how I hosted a successful webinar and then I actually hosted a successful webinar, I'd suddenly want to buy a bottle of wine or to do nothing but stare at the television or my phone. If I had a great day at work, I'd suddenly be eating *so much food* once I got home. As I mentioned in the previous chapter about finances, when I got a big paycheck or things were going well financially, I often felt like I had to spend all the money and get it away from me.

This pattern was a shocker when I finally began to see it. I was sabotaging my body and health on all fronts—not because things were wrong, but because things were right. What the hell?

This pattern ultimately stemmed from the underlying belief that I was fundamentally flawed and didn't deserve good things. This was such a hard thing to realize! No one wants to wake up to the fact that they think this way about themselves.

But, for me, facing this really was the first step. Accepting the truth of where I was really at—rather than the story I'd been telling myself—started a chain reaction for good.

Today, I still struggle with self-sabotage when things go right. But instead of just trying to gloss everything over and get to the part where I feel good and have success, I spend time in the fuzzy gray area where I write about how I'm able to feel my feelings, and then I try to, you know, *actually feel my feelings*. I acknowledge that there is part of me that is hugely uncomfortable when good things happen. I acknowledge that part of myself and accept that part of myself. I don't try to change that part of my story without spending time with it.

Body and Intimacy

When I didn't love my body, it made it very hard for me to let anyone get close to it.

My husband Rob and I have tons of chemistry, and romantically things have largely been great for us since we've been together. But when things started to fall apart with my novel-writing career and I gained weight, I wanted nothing to do with him.

Because I didn't love and accept myself, I couldn't fathom anyone else loving and accepting me—and certainly not in *that* way. I pulled away and distanced myself and let self-loathing take over everything.

The crazy thing is, Rob loves me beyond words. He thinks I'm sexy no matter what I weigh or what I wear. I am exceptionally lucky in this regard. I snagged a good one, let me tell you.

But because I was critical of my body and was seeing it through the lens of disappointment and anger, it broke the connection I had not just with myself, but with Rob, too.

True health and body acceptance will fuel relationships, while the inability to love and accept ourselves will disconnect us and distance us from others. This makes it critical for us to write a better story for ourselves in this area, because without healing, we risk damaging friendships, marriages, and any of our most precious relationships.

To try and heal this area, I wrote a lot in *Lara's Life* about how connected Rob and I felt to one another. I wrote about how we had a great sex life and how close we were. I also spent time talking to my therapist about this issue, because it's such a big one. I'm all about throwing every tool at a problem to ensure you get a solution, and therapy is one of the best tools around.

I'm happy to report that Rob and I have a better relationship than ever. We have slayed some major demons together this past year—and not just intimacy-related ones. The *Author Your Life* process showed me where we were disconnected in bigger ways. We were both on separate paths headed away from each other, and we needed to come back together. I'll talk more about this in the Ordeal section of the book.

How to Start Down a Path of Health in Mind and Body

Exercise #1: Accept Yourself as You Are Now

If the idea of better health seems overwhelming to you—you wonder how you'll start an exercise program, learn to meditate, stop drinking, let people get close to you, whatever it is—please know that your only job right now is not to do any of those things. Your job right now is to take a deep breath and just be who you are and accept who you are. This is you. This is where you are in your journey. It's not good or bad. It just is.

I'm not writing this book from a place of being fixed or being perfect. Sure, I've stopped drinking and lost weight, but I have a long way to go. Writing *Lara's Life* has helped me enormously, but I'm still in it. And any progress I've made on the outside is a reflection of changes that have occurred on the inside.

Practically speaking, that means that, every day, I have to accept where I'm at. I still want to do more growing and changing, but I can't do that without acknowledging the truth about my position now. Instead of fighting my body (i.e. creating a dam against the flow of the river), I'm accepting it (i.e. jumping into the river and letting it carry me where I need to go).

To accept where you are today, try writing the following sentences in your story:

[Your Name] loves and accepts her body right now, just as it is. She is willing to stop fighting herself. She connects with her body instead of trying to overcome it. [Your Name] is honest with herself. Her eyes are open to the ways in which she can see herself more positively. Her ears are open to the ways she can better listen to herself. Because of this, she feels more connected to her body and understands her body more fully.

You may also want to add a measure of gratitude into your story because gratitude is such a powerfully transformative practice. Think about the ways that your body works hard for you and helps you every single day. Picture in your mind how reliably your body shows up for you. Now, write a story where you acknowledge and appreciate your body. For example:

[Your Name] loves her body. She is thankful for her body and all that it does for her. She sees her body in the mirror and feels gratitude for all the ways her body works so hard on her behalf. She sees every curve, every bend, every scar and sends that part love and thanks.

Exercise #2: Listen to Your Body

I talked about this exercise earlier in the chapter, and this was a big one for me. It's not so much writing a better story as it is listening to the story our body is already telling us. It's deceptively simple.

Dear [Your Name],

This is your body. And this is what I want to tell you.

After you write that, keep your pen on the page and just see what comes up. I can almost guarantee you will be surprised at what words flow next.

Exercise #3: Paint that Picture

Now ask yourself: What does it look like when you are healthy inside and out? Do you have energy? Do you feel confident? Are you quick to laugh? Do you engage your friendships or relationships more readily?

As a follow-up, think about what you *do* when you are healthy inside and out. Do you leave the house more? Are you more intimate with your partner? Do you swim three times each week at the pool?

Now, as you've done in previous chapters, you'll

want to write a story where you are doing and feeling those things. Again, you don't have to put pressure on yourself to be Hemingway and write the greatest story of all time, ever. But give yourself permission to really imagine it and write it out. If you're having trouble, try answering the following questions: Where are you? How does it smell? Who are you with? What do you see?

For me, one of my favorite pictures of being healthy inside and out is being in northern Michigan and hunting for morel mushrooms. Those suckers are hard to find! And it means I'm in the woods for hours on end, hiking up hills and trekking this way and that for some fungi.

In my story, I feel so strong as I hike. I'm wearing clothes I feel great in. All around me is the green of the woods and the sound of wind in the trees. I am full of joy and gratitude because I've given myself permission to do a thing that I love. My mind is quiet, and my heart is full. I'm so thankful for the woods and for the opportunities I've been given.

Exercise #4: Get Those Feelings Involved Again

After you finish writing your story, put your hand on different parts of yourself and just say thank you and send love to that part of your body.

For example, place your hand on your arm and say how thankful you are for that arm and how hard it works. Now, place your hand on your foot and send that foot love for keeping you upright and for helping you get from point A to point B every day. You can even place your hand on your heart and just let yourself fill up with love for your body and all it gives you.

If this feels awful and forced, I totally get it. It was for me too when I first started. That's because I really didn't love my body at all. But "fake it 'til you make it" applies here, too, because our body doesn't know that we are forcing the emotions. It thinks they're real! In my case, my perspective on by body gradually began to change. Before long, I was actually feeling the love for my body, instead of forcing it.

There are some wonderful body meditations in the Resources section of this book that can help you begin to feel more gratitude, love, and acceptance toward your body. If you don't know where to begin, having a practiced teacher take you through a short meditation can make a world of difference.

EIGHT

Meeting the Mentors

Holy crap, you guys! Congratulations! You're out of the Leap of Faith section of your journey, and you're in the Meeting the Mentors stage. High-five yourself Liz Lemon style because you are awesome.

I absolutely love this part of the journey because there is so much magic that happens here. In any story, the hero receives a guide who gives the hero indispensable advice and wisdom. This makes all the difference in the quest. Think Obi-Wan helping Luke in *Star Wars*, or Haymitch helping Katniss in the *Hunger Games*, or the magical animated objects helping Belle in *Beauty and the Beast*.

If you feel alone or on your own, the Meeting the Mentors section is going to rev you right up, because you're going to understand, without a doubt, that the universe has your back. This is the part of the story where the universe sends us exactly the help we need.

When I started *Lara's Life*, I was shocked by the

resources that came my way exactly when I needed them. And although the Meeting the Mentors section technically comes after Answering the Call and the Leap of Faith, I want to tell you that help arrived for me almost immediately—so, really, this part of your journey can happen any time.

As I mentioned in the Leap of Faith: Achieving Financial Abundance section, one of the first people who showed up for me was Denise Duffield-Thomas, who is a great teacher about money.

At the very start of January 2018, I started watching Denise's videos and downloading every freebie I could from her website and reading her books—you name it, I did it.

To be clear, Denise lives in Australia, so obviously she wasn't an in-person mentor for me, but she may as well have been. Her webinars and books and resources made it feel like she was right there in the room with me, helping me every step of the way.

I've connected to so many other mentors in this manner. Ash Ambirge, Marie Forleo, Cheryl Strayed, heck, even Oprah—these are all people who had something to teach me, and I could access them all through my laptop while sitting at my kitchen table.

Which brings me to an important point. We live in a world where digital technology can connect us to people who are halfway around the globe. It's incredible, and it's something we can all take advantage of. There are so many amazing experts out there who are putting resources online and sharing their knowledge—

women, especially, are doing this more and more. Your mentor could be a mouse click away.

Your mentor could also be a book. Or a documentary. Practically speaking, some of your mentors might be people who you engage professionally. My therapist, for example, could fall under the heading of a mentor. In the past I've hired a life coach as well—someone who I knew had the expertise I needed. I've paid to join online mastermind groups, and I've attended conferences and retreats where the speakers and other conference-goers have given me exactly the wisdom I needed in the moment.

It doesn't matter whether you meet your mentor in person or write them a check to help you or engage them on the page or through a screen. Your job is to believe that they're out there, keep your eyes open for them, and be open to what they're telling you.

We Need Other People, Yo

As a writer, I understand what solitary work is like. I absolutely get what it means to hole up by yourself and shut out the world and just work. As I try to think about a more solitary job than being a writer, lighthouse keeper comes to mind, but that's about it.

Even as a writer, though, I know how much I need other people in the process of producing a book. I need beta readers to review early drafts and help me understand where I'm going wrong. I need critique groups to bounce ideas off of. I need copyeditors to proofread every word.

If, in writing, one of the most solitary crafts imaginable, other people are still required to get the job done, then I think it's safe to say that pretty much *every* endeavor needs other people. Certainly your work writing a better story needs other people.

This might be hard to hear, especially for people who are highly introverted or who don't like engaging with other people in general. In an increasingly disconnected world, it may be easy to dismiss needing others —but, unfortunately, the Hero's Journey can't be successful for anyone who tries to go it alone the whole time.

Who are Mentors, and What do they Do?

We're going to keep the definition of a mentor simple here. Mentors can help us in a ton of ways but, at its simplest, a mentor delivers an idea, information, or inspiration when we need it. Some mentors hang around for a long time and can help you for years, but that's not a requirement. Mentors might be in and out of your life in a flash once their job is done. The mentor delivers what you need, and your role is to accept the help.

Which brings me to an important point. I had a friend who first sent me a link to Denise Duffield-Thomas, but it sat in my inbox for ages. Even though the help was right there, it was my job to click it and learn. It was my job to find the right life coach and hire that person. Same with my therapist—I had to actively search them out and engage their services. I had a role to play in getting the information I needed from my mentor, and you will too.

The good news is that the universe makes it easy for us to get the help we need. There will be prompts and signs and whispers inside our hearts. But at the same time, neither the universe nor the mentor is going to do the work for us. Gandalf couldn't throw the ring into Mount Doom for Frodo. He was just there to help and guide—not do the heavy lifting.

In the Resources section of this book, you'll find authors, teachers, and podcasters whom I consider mentors. Every one of those resources popped up in my path when I needed it. But no one could read the books for me or go through the hard stuff on my behalf. That was all me.

Signs and Wonders

Objects can sometimes be as powerful as people, and they can guide us, too. During that first year of writing *Lara's Life*, I was having a tough time at the start of the year. As I mentioned earlier in the book, our financial picture was bleak, I was drinking quite a bit, and I had lost a sense of purpose after my novel-writing career had petered out.

That's when an awesome woman who I spent a day with at a retreat told me to get a talisman. As she described it, a talisman is a physical object that embodies the truth of who I am and I'm headed. She showed me her talisman, which was a lightning bolt necklace, because she is a force of nature and it was a reminder of that.

When I thought about it and sat with this idea, I felt like inside of me there was a bright diamond—that my future was sparkling and beautiful—and I just had to believe it and bring it to light.

Now, I wasn't sure what my talisman was, and I knew full well I couldn't afford a diamond, but I figured that whatever I *could* afford would find me, and the right talisman would come into my life. I was in New York at the time, so I wandered around a section of Brooklyn on a dreary day. It was spitting rain and blowing wind, but I knew there was a bright, glittering talisman calling to me.

I popped into store after store, but nothing I looked at felt right. Some stores I ruled out because the clerks were total snobs, and I didn't want that energy on whatever I bought. Finally, in the eleventh hour, as I was just about to give up my quest, I walked down a set of cement steps into a quiet little store where a woman was behind the counter making jewelry. It was clearly her store, and these were her designs. She smiled and welcomed me.

Right away, I knew my talisman was there. And sure enough, I found a delicate gold necklace with a little circle of tiny, sparkling crystals. It wasn't diamonds, but it was perfect. It was also exactly in my price range.

That's when I looked up and saw the store's name. Until then, I didn't realize where I was. When I saw the name, goose bumps crawled up my neck, and I nearly started crying. The store was called "Written."

At that point, *Author Your Life* was just a gauzy idea I had; it was barely anything I could talk about yet. But when I saw the name of the store, I knew I was supposed to keep going with this idea and bring it to life. Every day that I wore my talisman, I could feel the universe cheering me on and rooting for me. The universe totally had my back, and the talisman was proof. When I felt like I wanted to give up, I drew power from my talisman. I let it help me and encourage me and become another mentor on my journey.

How to Fill Your Journey With Kick-Ass Mentors

Exercise #1 – Write and Ye Shall Receive

If you need or want a mentor, all you have to do is ask. First, think about what you need help with most. In my case, my finances were so screwed up, it's no surprise that my first mentor was a financial teacher.

Think about the areas where you are struggling. What questions would your mentor help you answer? How would you feel when you got the information you needed?

Try writing a scene where you have the mentor you need and they are giving you exactly the help you imagined. Don't worry about the specifics of who the mentor is or what form they take—just focus on what information you get and how you feel. For example:

[Your Name] finds the perfect mentor at the perfect time. This mentor gives incredible help and guidance about [spe-

cific issue here]. When [Your Name] gets the information she needs, she feels safe, energized, and enlightened. [Your Name] knows the universe has her back, and that the right teachers will always come at the right time.

If you know there is a specific resource you need to access your mentor, such as a class or a workshop, then write a story where you have the funds and ability to take advantage of that opportunity. Picture yourself there, and write about it in as much detail as you can.

Exercise #2 – Look and Listen

Your mentors are out there, and the good news is that you don't have to worry about how they get to you. You don't have to imagine the form they take or put your name on a big billboard so they can find you. That's the universe's job, so you're off the hook! Your only job is to recognize your mentors when they show up.

It can be useful to write a story where you make sure you can see them, since mentors sometimes hide in plain sight. Some signs that your mentor might be nearby are coincidences, symbols, and a gut feeling. Here's how you can write a story around making sure you see your mentor(s):

[Your Name] has her eyes opened to seeing her mentors. Her ears are attuned to anything they might say, and she knows when her mentors speak. [Your Name] is open to coincidences or other occurrences that point her in the direction she needs to go.

Similarly, have you ever noticed that certain patterns

or themes or words pop up in your life from time to time? For example, when it was time for me to put pen to paper and start writing this book, I kept seeing and hearing messages of "voice" around me. About raising my voice, using my voice, how the world needs my voice, etc. Everywhere I looked, it was like I saw and heard the universe shouting that it was time to *start writing already*, and to say what I needed to say.

When you look at your life, are there themes that pop up over and over? These could be words or images, but they might also be messages. Are different people telling you the same thing again and again, for example that you should try something or do something?

If so, try writing the following story:

[Your Name] recognizes patterns in her life that are trying to speak to her and get her attention. She takes the action she is supposed to when these patterns pop up. Her heart knows what to do, and she acts in alignment with it.

Exercise #3 – Find Your Talisman

My talisman made such a difference in my life, and I believe there are talismans out there for everyone who wants one. If you're ready to find yours, write a story where that happens! Think about what you feel when you wear your talisman. Do you have a form you'd love it to take—maybe a ring or necklace or even a tattoo? How does your talisman help and guide you? Mine reminds me constantly that a better story is possible, and that even though I sometimes felt like a lump of coal, I have a bright diamond of a future just waiting for me. Whatever your talisman is and whatever it does for you, you can write a story about it starting today. I can't wait for you to find it!

CHANGE

NINE

Cha-Cha-Change: The Big Picture

Welcome to the part of the Hero's Journey where the hero (again, that's totally you) finds out what they're made of. This is exciting, awesome stuff! It's also where the universe is going to get all up in your face and ask you how bad you want that new story you're writing for yourself. The answer needs to be "a lot," or at least enough to outweigh the difficult times when they come. Because if you're trying to grow and change, challenges *will* arise. As vulnerability expert Brené Brown puts it, "I've never seen any evidence of how-to working without talking about what gets in the way."

Chances are, in the process of writing your new stories in the last section, some feelings might have cropped up for you that were raising a big red flag embroidered with, "Hey wait, I'm not sure I like this!" Maybe it was fear or guilt or shame or confusion or anger or something else entirely. Our goal isn't to write a story where we don't have these feelings, but rather to accept them when they come and see what they're trying to tell us. Chances are, those feelings are going to crop up even more in the Change section.

According to our roadmap, the Change section contains two parts: the Road of Trials, and the Ordeal. Sounds fun, right?

I'm going to guess some folks will just skip over this part entirely. But I'm here to tell you that there's plenty of good that happens in this part of the journey. I spent most of the last year being in a state of Change, and I wouldn't trade it for anything. This part of the process made me stronger and gave me more courage. I cut way back on drinking. Rob and I became closer. Our finances got sorted out. And I found the courage to start writing this book.

Ultimately, I became more connected to my highest self and stopped living a numb life. In the midst of many storms—financial, emotional, physical—there were so many clouds with silver linings. For every challenge the universe threw at me, it also sent along plenty of love. There were moments when I felt lonely, but never alone. The universe had my back the whole time, and it has yours, too.

That's because, in any story, this is the part where we root hardest for the hero, and the universe is rooting for you, too.

One of my favorite movies from this past year is *Avengers: Infinity War*, and I can't get enough of the character of Thor. Not just because he's played by an insanely hot Hemsworth (though that doesn't hurt), but because of what he loses in his journey. At the start of the film, he suffers incredible personal loss, not to mention the destruction of his community of people from Asgard. He's on an impossible quest to make a weapon that will defeat the villain in the film, Thanos. He pretty much dies making the weapon, and there's this all-is-lost moment when you wonder if he's even going to live through the ordeal.

Thankfully, Thor is resurrected by the weapon's power, and that willingness to suffer and endure so much gives him incredible strength by the end of the film. It's because of what he's been through—*not* in spite of it—that he can be so powerful. And it's the same for us, too.

Change is here to show us where we're out of alignment. The two parts of Change—the Road of Trials and the Ordeal—are where we see clearly how the story we're writing is in conflict with the one we are living. It's like a huge oak tree saying it needs to get through a tiny door. So the universe is like, "Cool, I can make that happen for you, but it's going to take some trimming."

Our job in this process is to keep writing the story we want to have happen, even as we, the oak trees, get trimmed up by the universe.

How to Use this Part of the Book

At the end of each section, you'll see more questions than writing prompts. Thanks to the Awareness section, you already know how to write your story. **Now, your job is to question and examine what's coming up for you as you engage your journey.**

These are guided questions to help you respond to

what you're experiencing. And since everyone's experience is different, it's all about reflecting on what's happening to you. I've focused on questions and prompts because it's up to *you* to decide how to respond when the River Sucks comes rushing at you. You can fight it and rage and say, "Why me?" and try desperately to stop its flow. Or you can surrender to it and go along with it and say, "Okay, this is hard, but I'm willing to experience this. It's not going away, and I can't fight it, so that means I have something to learn from it."

The flow is change. The flow is how we arrive at a happy ending.

TEN

The Road of Trials

The Road of Trials is where external challenges can help us see the places we're out of synch with ourselves and need some adjustments. (The Ordeal, by contrast, comprises more emotional self-reflection. It's less about what happens around us or to us, and more about what happens inside of us.)

There could be a hundred thousand ways that this disparity manifests, and a hundred thousand things that the universe wants to teach any one of us. But here are some of the primary reasons we might experience trials.

Unrealistic Expectations

One of the biggest areas in which I see people out of alignment is when they are trying to meet unrealistic expectations—whether someone else's or society's—instead of staying true to their own hearts. This can cause conflicts and trials in spades.

Let's say you have a calling in your heart to be a veterinarian, but your parents want you to go into the family insurance business. In your effort to please your parents and seemingly avoid conflict, you may think the right course of action is to do as they ask. But to be out of alignment with your heart and your true calling is a recipe for disaster. You may feel sad, even depressed. You might have anxiety because you're so far out of sync with what you want to be doing. And the business might not even prosper because a.) you hate being there and b.) the universe doesn't even want you there, so it's not going to make things easy for you. This could manifest in hundreds of different ways including lost clients, health problems, issues with colleagues, financial difficulties, and much more.

The idea that you should (or shouldn't) do something because someone else thinks they know what's best for you is like saying you love butterflies and surrounding yourself with cockroaches instead.

Are there areas of your life where you are listening to expectations instead of listening to yourself? This pressure can come from family, friends, or even yourself. We are sometimes our own worst advice givers!

For example, for the longest time I told myself that I "should" lose weight. The idea that I should be skinnier came from a place inside me that was out of alignment —an old, broken part of my heart that thought I was worthless if I was a size 16, instead of knowing that I was awesome no matter what weight I was. Also, society pretty much screams this at women all the time, every day, in commercials, magazines, beauty products, you name it. So it's no wonder that so

inadequate just because we're not a size ze

"Should" told me to shed the fat, and I w

stories in *Lara's Life* to that end, i.e. lots of wor

tune of "Lara loses weight." But alignment said t

on loving myself, and my stories in *Lara's Life* bec

more about being kind and compassionate to myse

"Should" made going to Weight Watchers—and failing

at it every time—a slog and a trial. Alignment made it

so that I had more love for myself, which helped reduce

my suffering and made me less inclined to want to stuff

myself with carbs and cheese. (For more on this, please

see the chapters The Leap of Faith: Loving Yourself and

The Leap of Faith: Connecting to Your Body and

Health.)

To write a story where you tune out "should" and

tune into your heart, think about the following

questions:

- Are there areas where you feel out of
  alignment, where you're trying to make
  someone else happy, or listening to an old
  tape looping through your head that just isn't
  true anymore? If so, make a list of those
  places. Then imagine—and write!—what a
  better story for yourself would be in those
  areas.

- What's one thing you would do today if
  everyone's expectations for you were lifted?
  Write a few sentences where you get to do
  that thing.

tening to what's really in
back to the Answering
ook, and do exercise

many of us feel
o.
rote lots of
ds to the
focus
ame
lf.

with the Right People

ʋr another podcast I love, *My Favorite*
, often talk about how they go to therapy
sessions together. This is because they not only need to learn how to keep communicating effectively with each other, but also because the problems and issues they face are so unique to their situation. Issues with the podcast community, snags with their multi-city tours, big financial changes—I'm sure they go through a lot of trials together that few others will ever experience. One of the hosts, Karen, called it "rare air," as in not a lot of people can relate to their experiences.

I've thought about this phrase a lot as Rob and I try to do ambitious and life-changing things. Starting businesses. Writing books. Actively trying to become better people. Sometimes, it feels like a lonely place. We've both lost friends along the way who'd rather we stay small and gossip over drinks.

You may have people in your life who aren't exactly cheerleading the changes you're making. They could be talking behind your back or they could be telling you outright that what you're aiming for is ridiculous, that you can't do it, or saying that *people like you* don't get lives like *that*. They could be questioning why you need that new gym membership, why you seem so much happier, or asking you who you think you are to deserve such things. These could be people who are close to you. They could be family. They might be people you love. But that doesn't make them right.

One of the ways that our Road of Trials gets easier is by surrounding ourselves with the right people on the journey. Not just mentors and guides, but allies who can hold our hand and give us encouragement and cheer us the whole way.

Your Road of Trials may be showing you some people from whom you might need to distance yourself, or with whom you need to limit your exposure. It's time to identify anyone in your life who is belittling you or flat-out doesn't believe in you. The goal is to find a way to not listen to those naysayers and instead listen to a.) your heart and b.) the people who know you're a rock star.

To write a story where you're surrounded with the right allies, think about the following questions:

- What do the people in your life who support you say and do? When you write your story about these people, it might bring to mind people who do the opposite—those who don't support you and perhaps even belittle you. Are there ways you can distance yourself from the latter group? If you need the universe to guide you, try writing: [*Your Name] is surrounded by the people she needs on her quest. Her eyes are open to see true allies, and she has healthy boundaries with people she's not supposed to align herself with.*

- Do you need more allies in your life? Write a story where the right people come into your life and they support you one hundred percent. What do they say? How do they make you feel?

Your Friend Failure

When my novel-writing career imploded, it happened so, so spectacularly.

For years, I'd been working on a young-adult novel that I felt amazing about. I loved this book, and often called it "the book of my heart."

When I finally submitted this book to my editor, she decidedly did *not* feel the same way. I tried revising the book, but ultimately the disconnect between what I was writing and what she wanted was so big that the publisher actually released me from my contract. In other words, it was easier to have me walk than keep me around.

So much ouch, you guys.

At almost exactly the same time, my romance publisher decided they didn't want me around either. I'd fulfilled my contract with them and produced several books—one of which was even nominated for a major award. They were great books and I felt awesome about them. But the sales numbers for these books just weren't there.

I was willing to take less money to continue working with this publisher, or to try a new series under a new name, but my romance publisher wanted none of it. They sent me packing and closed the door on me abruptly and permanently. My awesome agent tried selling my new romance to some other publishers, but they didn't want me either. Bad sales are like a stink you can't get off you—and no one wants to touch you as a result.

This left me reeling. My whole life, I'd only ever wanted to be a novelist. It's the only career path I'd ever imagined for myself. When I was little, I had a house picked out for myself based on the fact that it had the view I wanted when I sat down to write. Now, here I was, feeling like I no longer knew how to write books for a living. My identity was in shambles. Who was I?

Eventually, I decided I didn't need a publisher's permission to write a book.

I'm still a writer, I thought. *Because a writer just writes.*

I resolved to pen a new book no matter if it was publishable or not. I still had my job at the University of Michigan, so it's not like Rob and I were dependent on a book contract. I was going to return to novel writing for the joy of it. For the pure love of it. Fuck publishing.

The problem was, I didn't have another novel in me.

My muses, which had until then been whispering book ideas at me constantly, were suddenly quiet. I didn't have any inspiration. I sat down to write a few things, but they were forced and felt awful. I kept trying to pound something out, until my husband begged me to stop and just sit in whatever it was that I was going through. *Sit in the darkness*, as he put it.

Yeah, screw that, I thought. I wasn't so good at sitting. I wanted to be *doing*.

So I kept trying. I penned some erotica. I took another stab at a young-adult book. Nothing felt right, and nothing was working. I felt like a complete failure.

Ultimately, I decided that maybe I'd take a break from novel writing and I'd start my own business. I wrote about this business idea in the Leap of Faith: Discovering Your Purpose section of the book, and there was so much that was great about this idea. I believed it could work. I threw all my eggs into this business basket, and then the basket went tumbling over a metaphorical business sea wall, crashing into the ocean, yolks and shell mixing with the storming waves. It was a disaster.

First my book, and now my business. These were such big failures! I felt like everything I put my hand to sucked ass.

And yet.

The process of both of those failures led me to imagine what I could do to turn things around. It led me back to stillness, to the first part of the Hero's Journey. It led me back to Answering the Call and asking what I was here to do. It led me to wonder what would happen if I wrote a better story for myself—*literally*—and tried to affect the outcome of my own journey.

Both of those failures led me straight to *Author Your Life*.

And no matter what happens with this book—if I

never sell a single copy—I know its power and I believe in it. I will always be writing in *Lara's Life* because this journey has changed me. I believe that discovering the *Author Your Life* concept has been my calling all along. I believe so deeply in this work that I will do it no matter if there is a paycheck or a publisher or a website or *anything*.

That sense of purpose and rightness feels like an incredible gift. It feels like a gift that was given to me in a box built entirely out of failure. How awesome is that? I wouldn't have the gift if it weren't for the failure. I am grateful to the failure. I know what a great teacher failure can be.

There are countless stories out there of people who have bombed in a big way, and that crisis is what led them to success. Walt Disney's first animation studio went bankrupt before he started his own. Oprah was fired from a broadcasting job for getting "too involved" in a story before she launched her empire built around intimacy with other people's stories. J.K. Rowling was divorced and bankrupt when she began writing *Harry Potter*.

The Hero's Journey is a circle for a reason. There's never a place where it ends, and there's never a place where you can't begin anew. So launch yourself into a thing and try something! Take the leap. If it fails and you have trials that are just too big to overcome, then you simply go back to Answering the Call and you sit in stillness. You listen to your heart and you adjust. You try again. What you learn and what you discover will lead you to the right thing at the right time.

Because failure is never an end, just a new beginning.

To write a story where you make friends with failure, think about the following questions:

- Is failure trying to teach you something? You may be writing a story where you overcome obstacles when the universe is telling you to just turn around and walk away from the obstacles because you're on the wrong path. If you need wisdom in this area, write: *[Your Name] sees the path that she should be on. She understands clearly which direction she should go. The universe shows her and helps her.*

- Where in your life are you scared to fail? And/or is there a situation in the past where you've failed, and that's made you anxious to try something again? Perhaps you need a new story where you're full of courage and moxie.

- Can you sit with your fear and allow it to be there? Instead of trying to kick it to the curb and make it go away, can you acknowledge that it's just part of the journey? That it's not good or bad—it just is? It might be trying to show you something, and you can always write a story where your eyes are open to see what it's trying to show you.

- Write a story where, even if you try something and fail, you still love yourself, the people who are meant to be in your life still believe in you, and you're able to try again.

Are you Choosing Your Trials?

I appreciate rules and generally like to follow them. One rule that I try to abide by is that our cars have their oil changed every 3,000 miles. And for a long time, there was part of me that expected Rob to be on top of this because I guess I just thought that oil changes were his job.

What this meant is that when it was time for my car to have its oil changed, I'd pissily (yes, *pissily*) take it to the shop and resent the fact that I had to do this, when *clearly* it was Rob's job. And by clearly, I mean we never talked about it and it this was just an expectation I had pulled out of thin air. There were even times when I took Rob's car in because I knew it was over on its mileage. If someone had invented a Resent-o-Meter at that moment, mine would have been red-lining. I was so angry that Rob wasn't taking care of the cars *like he was supposed to*.

Oh, the drama that stemmed from this! I created a whirlwind of bad energy, fights, and resentment all because I'd made up a dumb rule in my head about who was in charge of oil changes. It took me a long time to figure out that if I just *did the oil changes* because it was important to me, there would be so much less fighting and fewer "trials."

Wrong thinking is an insanely fast track to trials.

And sometimes, it's hard to believe that *we're the ones* welcoming bad stuff into our lives. It could be allowing fights and resentment to create a toxic mushroom cloud inside the relationship, as was my case with the oil changes, or it could be much worse. Choosing to continue to drink, for example, could have led me to major health trials down the road. I know plenty of women who keep choosing bad men, and this brings tons of drama and awfulness into their lives. I know people who are so afraid of changing jobs that they are staying in horrible work situations that compromise their integrity and could be categorized as borderline abusive. I know people who are on the verge of an affair because they refuse to acknowledge how unhappy they are in their relationship and to just deal with the truth of that.

The goal isn't to be perfect, but rather to see where our thinking or our choices are holding the door open for trials to waltz right in. In other words, the trials you're experiencing could be universe-sent, but they might also be *you*-sent.

For me, the hardest part about coming to terms with self-made trials is that they can be a welcome distraction. When we create a fire of chaos in our lives, that fire becomes our focus. We have to put it out immediately. It can give us purpose. It can even make us feel closer to people. All hands on deck! We are going to do this thing together!

I once worked for a boss who loved to create drama and emergencies. I believe this happened because she was terrified of thinking strategically and looking ahead. She needed to focus on the here and now, so she blew things up in order to have an immediate problem for her team to fix. She created trials for that office every day and, ironically, it did give us focus for a time. It made my colleagues and me closer because we were constantly doing battle in the trenches together. But after a while, it was exhausting. Ultimately, the office became a very miserable place.

To write a story where you no longer choose drama and trials, think about the following questions:

- If you are experiencing trials right now, ask yourself if there are areas of your life where you're not facing something or looking at a problem honestly. Are you blind to your own role in the trials, and are you inadvertently welcoming drama into your life? Write a story where you see your life honestly and realistically, and where your eyes are open to the ways you need to change.
- Have you created "rules" that you expect people to follow, but you haven't shared these rules with those around you? Can you write a story where you let those rules or expectations go?
- Are you avoiding a tough choice or decision that will help alleviate drama in your life? What might happen if you face that decision head-on?

Upping Your Mad Skillz

Sometimes we experience trials because we just don't have the full set of skills or training that we need, and our butts take on some bruises while we master our craft.

For instance, I got the idea for my debut novel, *Donut Days,* in 1999. It would take *ten years*—a whole decade!—before the book hit shelves. Between 1999 and 2009, I had so much to learn: about how a book is structured, about how to find an agent, about how to write for teens, and so much more. And I received so many rejection letters along the way from editors and agents; I often joked that I could have wallpapered my bathroom with them.

I was extremely frustrated in this process. I wanted to be published so badly I could taste it. It was the biggest dream I'd ever had, and I was determined to make it work. But it wouldn't work—it *couldn't* work—until I mastered the skills I need to write an awesome book.

The trials along the way were often heartbreaking, but they always sent me back to a place of learning. I devoured how-to writing books. I attended workshops and conferences. I networked. I read books that were similar to the ones I wanted to write so I could see what successful authors were doing. I learned and worked and studied. And eventually, I got there.

To write a story where you get the skills you need, think about the following questions:

- Do you need training information to achieve

your dream? You don't have to worry about *how* it gets to you (how you afford it, for example, because the universe will help you figure it out), and you don't have to worry about what happens next. You just have to know the gaps in your training, and be open to receiving it. Can you write a story where that happens?

- Conversely, is there any chance you *think* you need training, education, and skills, but really that's just an excuse? There may be a situation in which you think you need a new degree or a fresh course or that next book, but you're actually ready now. Ask yourself: Are you using education and training as an excuse to not have to leap into your dream?

Seeing Doesn't Have to Be Believing

One morning, I woke up with a sentence running through my head: "I am pointing my pencil in a new direction." As fast as I could, I scribbled it down on a piece of paper so I wouldn't forget it. I still have that scrap of paper, and I look at that sentence all the time.

To me, these are incredibly powerful words, because they serve as a reminder that as long as we keep writing, the universe will help us create the stories we want to be true in our lives. The universe can't push my pencil if I tuck it away.

Sometimes, that means that I'll write a new story,

putting pencil (or pen) to paper until my hand cramps, but I won't see anything happen as a result. It's frustrating and maddening. In August, just past halfway mark in my first year of writing *Lara's Life*, I wrote the following in my journal:

I am NOT doing great. I feel like I'm going backwards. Is this part of it? The last four days have been awful, I'm feeling depressed and worthless and like things aren't changing. I'm wrestling with whether I should just get a full-time job and not do the whole variable income thing.

I was nearly ready to give up, ready to just get a full-time job at some boring office and forget I'd ever started the *Author Your Life* process. I felt like it was obviously bullshit. Here, I'd been doing it for eight months and I was still having trouble in so many areas. And yet, I couldn't—or wouldn't—put my pen down. I had to keep going.

A few weeks later, my journal entry says this:

I know I'm on a great path. And manifestations aren't the point. I mean, yes, manifestations are awesome, but the journey to get to those manifestations is about getting happy, getting connected, loving yourself, getting grateful, and doing the small things along the way.

What I was trying to articulate was a bone-deep knowledge that change was happening and good things were on the way, I just couldn't see it yet. This will likely be true for you, too.

The universe is shifting things in our favor, lining up the chessboard for the perfect move, long before we can see it come to pass. When it came to our finances, I remember the moment when it finally felt like things

were going to start to getting better. It was November—
it took eleven months! But I remember when I could
feel the energetic shift happening. At the time, our bank
accounts were not any different, and nothing on the
outside indicated that our financial picture was less
bleak. But I knew, deep down, that things were on the
upswing. Today, our finances are markedly different,
and we are in a much healthier and better position with
our money. We're not where we want to be—I'm still
writing that story—but thank God we're not where we
were.

When I look back on it now, I realize that the whole
time I was writing a better financial story for myself, the
universe was working behind the scenes, helping it
come to pass. Even when things fell apart with our
money, it was all designed to help us get to a better
place. (For more on this, please read the Leap of Faith:
Achieving Financial Abundance chapter).

My point is that you can't always see how the
universe is working or what it's doing, but there might
be energetic shifts occurring in your favor, behind the
scenes. Your breakthrough is on its way, and just
because it's not manifesting yet doesn't mean your new
story isn't working. So stay with it and, above all, keep
writing.

To write a story where you keep the faith that the
universe has your back, think about the following
questions:

- Are there areas where you have peace, even
  though things look chaotic on the outside?

What is your heart telling you about these areas?

- Are you at a place where you're ready to give up? If so, before you throw in the towel, ask yourself: Are there internal changes you've been making so external stuff can come to pass? If so, *keep going*. Your breakthrough might be closer than you think.

The Simple Stuff

There are some simple and practical things we can all do to try and reduce the trials and ordeals in our lives. These are important options to consider because, chances are, you might need a combination of things to help your story improve. That's because no single solution is a magic bullet—even this book.

I am engaged in some aspect of the options below at all times. I'm not saying you have to do the same, but each of them is worth considering as a complement to all the amazing work you're doing as you write the book of your life:

- Journaling: There is scientific data about the benefits of journaling, which is a powerful tool. Journaling can help us examine what's holding us back or experiences in the past that have given us a story we need to revise. (Think of journaling as writing by looking backwards, whereas *Author Your Life* is writing by looking ahead.) We need both!

- Meditation: I've talked about this throughout the book, and I can't recommend it enough. Quieting your mind and making time for stillness is essential. I provide meditations in the Resources section that have helped me immensely.

- Exercise: I know, I know. You've heard it a bazillion times, but even if you just start small, it can make a huge difference in your physical and mental condition.

- Therapy: Ima keep hammering this one home. Talking to a trained professional is such a gift. If you can't afford to see someone in person, there are now apps that reduce the cost of connecting with someone. Therapy has changed my life.

- Reading: You've picked up this book so I assume you're a reader, which is awesome, and I want to encourage you to keep cracking those spines. There are so many incredible teachers out there, and I've listed some of my faves in the Resources section. The truths they write about dovetail with this work beautifully.

- A vision board: In addition to writing down what you desire to have in your life, make a picture of it, too. I did this to incredible effect —many things on my vision board came to pass quickly after I created it. One in particular was our little dog, Muenster. I had always wanted a little dog and made that part of the board I made in January 2018. Within six weeks, we had her, and she is *perfect*.

- Set Goals: In *Lara's Life*, I'd write my story on the right side of the page and my goals on the left. I wrote out the goals every day so I could keep them top of mind. It was so amazing when goals like "Lara loves herself" started coming true. I had financial goals on there as well. I broke them into short- and long-term categories, and they became like a documented record of how everything was changing.

ELEVEN

The Ordeal

In the previous chapter, I addressed external trials that might come our way as we write a better story for ourselves. Now, for the Ordeal, the universe is challenging us to look *inside* ourselves and face what's there. The Ordeal involves death (though only a symbolic one, I swear) and change.

At this stage in the game, we've already done a ton of work. In some ways, our stories might already be successful. Change is happening. But in order for us to keep going, the universe is going to force us to look inside ourselves and do battle with what's there.

In the *Wizard of Oz*, for example, Dorothy has faced trials to get the witch's broomstick and see the wizard. Now, she must look inside herself and finally realize that there's no place like home.

Face to Face with Myself

For me, the Ordeal involved facing fear and dropping an old identity. In my case, I had to look closely at how I was behaving and ask if that was really who I wanted to be.

In particular, this meant getting brutally honest about the ways I was holding Rob at arm's length. First, I was distancing myself from him because I was scared to be intimate. And second, I was distancing myself from him because, as the sole breadwinner, I was resentful that he wasn't contributing to our household income. I was angry and frustrated that all the bills and all the financial responsibility were falling to me (even though intellectually I understood that he had started a small brick-and-mortar ice cream business, and that those take at least a couple years to become profitable).

I was pulling away and letting fear and bitterness create an impenetrable wall around my heart. This was tough to face and acknowledge, because in some ways, behaving this way was very comfortable. My mom did this to my dad all the time, so I knew the pattern. It fit like a glove. It also meant I didn't have to expose myself in bed at a time when I felt incredibly vulnerable, and I could continue throwing myself into work, trying to pay the bills, shouldering it all like Atlas with a bad attitude.

But I could feel that this wasn't who I wanted to be. I knew I wanted a healthy marriage and to fix this. I wanted to feel like I had a teammate, not like I was carrying around a ball and chain that I resented.

Yet it was incredibly painful to write about this in *Lara's Life*. It was the most embarrassing, most humiliating, most shit-or-get-off-the-pot thing I had to face, and such a big part of me wanted to just pretend like everything was okay and it wasn't a big deal. Even now, everything inside me wants to find a way around putting it into this book because it's just so mortifying.

But I knew that keeping it to myself and pretending everything was okay would lead to disaster. So I pulled on my big girl panties and faced facts.

I had to write about how I wanted to have sex—even though I *so* didn't want to be intimate.

I had to write about how my heart was soft—even when I wanted to rage at the perceived injustice of me bearing all the financial weight for our home.

I had to write about how well we communicated—when all I wanted to do was shut Rob out.

I wrote about these things very crudely. If I'm honest, there wasn't much storytelling here. It's a lot more like a series of affirmations, because I just couldn't paint the picture. It was too hard. Here is an excerpt from *Lara's Life* at this point in the journey:

Lara finds ways to speak to Rob about their finances and what is happening there. They make a plan together. Lara lets no root of bitterness take hold, but approaches every situation with vulnerability and love. She trusts Rob's work is making a difference and will lead to good things. She trusts Rob and feels love and respect for him. She feels physically attracted to him, and lets her guard down so they can be intimate.

Author Your Prayer

Even though I was writing all these things, I still felt so alone in this part of the process. I wanted to believe change was possible, but part of me also knew I couldn't do it on my own. On the very next page of *Lara's Life* is a prayer I wrote to the universe. It was a cry for help.

Please, universe, help me not be bitter about Rob but to approach everything from a place of vulnerability. I can't look at everything through the lens of "it's not enough." Please help me find a way to not be scared. I feel so disempowered sometimes. Please help me put all this into perspective. Please help me be kind and not hard-hearted. Please help me be compassionate and loving. Please help me see all of Rob, not just what he "isn't" doing.

If you are feeling alone and that all your options are up, please put your pen to paper in prayer. And yes, it's okay if this one is in first-person. Just pour out what's in your heart. Ask the universe for help, because I promise you, there is a force out there that wants what's best for you. You don't have to put a name on who you're talking to, you don't have to convert to anything. Just write. Ask for help. The universe is listening.

Keep Your Pen Out

I would love to tell you that things changed right away and it was super easy, but of course that didn't happen. What did happen is that I kept my pen out—I didn't put away *Lara's Life* when things got hard, and I kept believing that a new and better story was possible.

I also understood where I was in the Hero's Journey. This part of the story was so impossibly, unbelievably difficult that it could only be the Ordeal. I knew if I could make it through this part, things would get better. This is true for you, too. If you're in the darkest part of the story, don't run from it. Stick with it. Stay long enough to understand this part of yourself and what it's trying to show you.

The Ultimate Surrender

When things finally began turning around, it was partly because I finally decided to invite the outcome I had been fighting against for so long. For instance, I had so much deep-seated fear about intimacy. But I finally decided that instead of waiting for a moment when I didn't feel the fear, I'd welcome the fear and just make it part of the process. I'd say, "I feel you, fear, and I'm done fighting you. You don't have to be gone for me to be intimate with Rob."

Instead of trying to fight against the financial challenges in my business, I decided to embrace them. I thought, "If I'm on the wrong track, I will face it and let the business go if that's what needs to happen." Indeed, that was exactly what needed to happen. Looking back now, I can see how out of alignment I was with the work, and yet all that I learned and experienced helped me build and launch *Author Your Life.* In other words, nothing we go through is useless or wasted—it can all contribute to what's next.

I think many of us are familiar with this tale of surrender, and the idea that the moment we give up what we think we want, we get what we need.

I have a close friend who, when she graduated from

business school, started applying for her dream job in the place she wanted to live most: New York City. She networked. She polished her resume. She nailed interviews and came so close to getting so many jobs—but never quite sealed the deal. Months went by. She just couldn't land anything. Finally, she put up her hands up in surrender. She told the universe: "This is what I want, but if it's not what you have in mind for me, that's okay. I'm open to whatever is next." She and her husband made plans to stay where they were, and to just sit tight.

Within a matter of weeks, she had an offer for her dream job in New York City. The universe just needed her to let go of the reins for a hot second and to trust that she didn't have to force open the door, that the right job would come along at the right time.

When you've done all you need to do, when you've fought until your last breath and you're absolutely exhausted, it's okay to put down your sword. It's okay to surrender. It's 100 percent cool to hand it over to the universe and say, "I need you to do this for me because I can't do it myself." That's a recipe for awesome things to happen next.

Takeaways

- Write the thing that scares you. Face the part of yourself you think you cannot.
- Author your prayer. Write and ask the universe to help you. Write that you can't do

it on your own, and trust that the universe will show up.

- Stay in your story. Don't put down your pen and walk away. Keep writing. This is all part of the Hero's Journey.
- When you've done everything you know to do, it's okay to surrender. Try giving up the thing you think you can't live without.

RENEWAL

TWELVE

Renewal, Heck Yeah!

At this stage in the Hero's Journey, your new story is coming true! This is so awesome, and not just for you—but for others as well.

That's because the first part of renewal is Transformation, when we ourselves are changed. But the other two parts, Endowment and Life Mastery, are all about *other people*. Endowment means using our new gifts and talents to teach and help others, and Life Mastery is leaving a legacy that truly makes the world a better place.

When we write a better story for ourselves, we can't help but make a positive impact. And not just on the people closest to us, such as our partner or our kids or our family or our friends, but people at work, people in our communities, and even people in different parts of the world.

The book *Author Your Life* exists because I wrote *Lara's Life* for an entire year. I didn't abandon my story, even as I went through excruciatingly difficult times, facing challenges both external and internal. Now, on the other side, I can share my journey. I'm choosing to do this in a very public way through a book. You might not want to write a book, but if you stay with the Hero's Journey, you will have something to teach others. You can't help but come through this process changed, with wisdom to impart.

In the Leap of Faith: Discovering Your Purpose section, I talked about how someone else is waiting on the other side of your transformation. I want to reiterate that here because sharing what we learn as we write a better story for ourselves is a huge part of the final phase of Renewal. Someone out there needs the wisdom you gain on your journey, and they need to hear it in the way *you* speak and share it. If you refuse your call and never write a better story for yourself, it has a ripple effect beyond just your own life.

Believe it or not, I still struggle with fear about sharing my experiences writing *Lara's Life*. I keep wondering what will happen if people think it's ridiculous. What if friends think I'm being disingenuous? What if people hate it and shame me online? But the call to share my story is bigger than my fear about what will happen if I do. I believe someone needs to read this book, so here I am! Fingers crossed, I hope it's you.

"Juicervose"

This book began with a story about a podcast, and it's going to end with a story about a podcast.

Here goes.

I was walking in the woods last summer, visiting a grove of poplars that I love to hang out in. They are near a rustic little cabin that my husband owned before we were married (think no running water, no indoor plumbing), and when we need to re-center ourselves, we always head to this cabin. I usually make a dash for the poplars once we're there.

There is something magical about these little trees. It always seems like their shimmery leaves are waving to me. And I often feel that the veil between the universe and me is ultra-thin in this grove.

Last summer, when I was there, I put my hand on one of the trees, and I heard a voice—as distinctly as someone speaking out loud—say the word "Juicervose."

Now, it was not only surprising to hear a voice speak to me from the middle of the woods where I was very much alone, but I also was confused by the word. I mean, I should say that I technically *knew* this word. "Juicervose" is an episode of another podcast that I love called *Radiolab*. I remembered the gist of the episode, which was about autism, but I couldn't fathom why the universe was speaking this word to me at this moment. What was going on?

Also—and this didn't cross my mind lightly—I wondered if I was going slightly crazy. Had I imagined the voice? What if I was suddenly hearing things in the woods?

But I trusted the magic of the poplars enough to give them the benefit of the doubt. So when Rob and I finally got back home to civilization, I cued up the "Juicer-vose" episode of *Radiolab* and gave it a listen. And yes, the episode is about autism. But more than that, it's about a family's journey to reach their son, Owen, who has autism, and to find a way to communicate with him. That way turned out to be Disney movies.

Owen's family realized that by acting out Disney movies and speaking as "characters," Owen could understand and interact with them more.

The *Radiolab* host, Jad Abumrad, has this exchange with Owen in the episode:

Jad: You're saying that when everyone was acting out the Disney movies, suddenly you could hear them better?

Owen: Right.

Jad: So when people would talk to you not *in the Disney movies, what do you remember about how they sounded?*

Owen: A little weird. Gibberish and rubbish.

Imagine the whole world being confusing and over-whelming, and then suddenly Disney movies are the translator you need to make everything understand-able. What a breakthrough.

One of the first movies that accomplished this for Owen was *The Little Mermaid*. As a kid, Owen would say the word "Juicervose" and, for the longest time, his family didn't understand it. Turns out, Owen was repeating the words of Ursula the sea witch when she tells Ariel that to get human legs it won't cost her much, "just your voice." This was Owen, telling his family that Disney movies *were his voice*.

When the poplars said the word "Juicervose," I think that what they were saying is that the information

I had to share about *Lara's Life*, and the particular way I shared it (i.e. my voice), was going to speak to someone in exactly the way they needed to hear it. Not everyone would get it. But some people would. I had to use my voice and share my story. Even if I was scared. Even if some people hated it. None of that mattered, because *Author Your Life* would be someone's Disney movie—and someone, somewhere, would be my "Owen."

The Story Cycle

I'm guessing that once I begin to publicly talk about *Lara's Life*, a new Hero's Journey is going to begin for me. One where I overcome even more fear. One where I might face bad reviews and online criticism, but I'll learn to do it from a place of love and vulnerability. One where I have to face another ordeal so a new, better Lara can emerge.

The reality is that the Hero's Journey never stops. We get through one cycle of it only to start another. The Hero's Journey is a circle for a reason. The universe will always ask us to keep growing, to keep stretching. There is never a part where we've mastered life one hundred percent. There's always something to learn and another person to help. There is always a better story we can write.

Which is all to say, keep putting pen to paper. Stick with the process. Don't tuck away your words and your voice and your story. Write it and live it and for goshsakes, *do* it.

Ready to begin the next chapter?

Me too.

Let's get to writing!

Resources

Meditations

These are all from the free Insight Timer app.

Loving Yourself

- Practicing Gentle Kindness Toward Ourself by Sarah Blondin
- Coming Home to Yourself Series by Sarah Blondin
- Heart Chakra Meditation by Sarah Jane Chapman
- 5-Minute Self-Love Meditation by Michelle Chalfant

Abundance

- Welcoming Abundance by Melody Litton
- Manifesting All You Desire by David Ji

Gratitude

- Litany of Thankfulness by Tony Brady
- The Gratitude Meditation by Michael Mackintosh

Books

Listed in alphabetical order by author.

- *The Gifts of Imperfection* by Brené Brown. Brené has a ton of awesome books, but this is by far my favorite. It's all about embracing imperfection and vulnerability.
- *The Science of Success: What Researchers Know that You Should Know* by Paula Caproni. This is a quick book about practical, research-based actions that can lead to success.
- *Get Rich Lucky Bitch* by Denise Duffield-Thomas. Oh man, do I love Denise! Clearing what she calls "money blocks" will also clear other blocks in your life, too. Her work is transformational on so many fronts.
- *Lucky Bitch* by Denise Duffield-Thomas. This one is great if you want a primer on how manifesting works, and how we really can make our own luck.
- *The Big Leap: Conquer Your Hidden Fear and Take Life to the Next Level* by Gay Hendricks. The book focuses on what the author calls the Upper Limit Problem, which is a form of self-sabotage when things go *right* in life. I had no

idea this was a thing I did! Now, I'm much more able to identify "upper limits" when they happen and move past them.

- *Learning to Love Yourself* by Gay Hendricks. This book helped me begin to understand what it meant to try and love myself, even on days when I wanted to beat myself up.

- *Loving What Is* by Byron Katie. Her four questions, which she calls "The Work," changed my thinking and helping me break free of old patterns. This book is amazing.

- *Wonder Over Worry: Move Beyond Fear and Doubt to Unlock Your Full Potential* by Amber Rae. This book is also writing-heavy in that it uses a ton of journal prompts to help readers get un-stuck. Rae shares her own story beautifully with an "I've been there" vibe I loved.

- *You Are a Badass* by Jen Sincero. This book will kick your butt and make you laugh the whole time. Sincero is a wonder. I felt like she was right there in the room with me on every page. This book is a must-have.

- *Tiny Beautiful Things: Advice on Love and Life from Dear Sugar* by Cheryl Strayed. The author's compassion for every single person who writes asking her advice is so beautiful, you can't help but want to have that same love for every soul. This book cracked my heart right open and took a meat tenderizer to it—in the best way possible.

Videos

- Oprah's *Super Soul Conversation* with Elizabeth Gilbert, "Finding Your Passion," October 2014. Gilbert speaks about the Hero's Journey and Answering the Call to Adventure.

Podcasts

- *By the Book*: I love this podcast not just because the hosts are awesome, but because if you're new to self-help, you can get a taste for it by listening to two other people read self-help and try to implement it. You still get great insights, plus a lot of belly laughs, so hashtag *winning*.
- *Dear Sugars*: Just like the book referenced above, but with two hosts (Cheryl Strayed and Steve Almond) and special guest experts who weigh in on the advice, too.
- *Oprah's SuperSoul Conversations*: I mean, natch. Oprah has incredible guests on her show, and the thread of transformation that runs through each episode is often sprinkled with just a tiny bit of magic.

Therapists

- *Psychology Today* has a good search function that can help you find a licensed therapist in

your area. Visit
psychologytoday.com/us/therapists

- The Talkspace app can connect you to a licensed therapist no matter where you live. It's much more affordable than traditional therapy. You can find the free app on your phone or visit talkspace.com

Note to Reader

I hope you've enjoyed reading *Author Your Life* as much as I've loved writing it! If you want to stay in touch and get the 411 on new courses, webinars, books, free stuff, and more, please sign up for my mailing list. Talk to you soon!

https://www.authoryourlifenow.com/join

About the Author

Lara Zielin is a published author, editor, and the founder of Author Your Life. Her debut young-adult novel *Donut Days* was selected to the Lone Star Reading List, and her romance novel *And Then He Kissed Me* (written as Kim Amos) was nominated for a Romantic Times Reader's Choice Award. Her magazine articles have appeared in *Writers Digest*, *Culture*, *Medicine at Michigan*, and more. She lives in Michigan with her husband and dog, and her goal is pretty much to eat ALL THE CHEESE.

Lara is represented by Susanna Einstein of Einstein Literary Management.

You can visit Lara on the web:

www.authoryourlifenow.com

Or follow her on Facebook at authoryourlife.

Pages

#20
#24
#26
#27
#31
#34
#44
#45
#47
#53
#62
#68
#69 *
#73 *
#78
#79
#81
#83
#84 X
#98
#99